"Harry Jackson is an emerging fresh voice whom God is raising up to open our eyes to the things Jesus is saying for our generation. *The Warrior's Heart* is a breakthrough work and will call us to the front lines to take our place to meet the enemy head on. It's clear the victory is already ours."

—Wellington Boone, founder and chief overseer,
Fellowship of International Churches, Atlanta

"If I were going to the front lines of a spiritual war zone, I would want Harry Jackson by my side and this manual in the hands of every soldier. It is clear-headed, full of wisdom, practical and quite dangerous to the forces of hell. If leaders and believers would take to heart the truths contained in every chapter, many needless casualties would be avoided and the purposes of God would be greatly advanced. On with it!"

—Dr. Michael L. Brown, president, FIRE School of Ministry,
Charlotte and New York

"Harry Jackson offers a rousing charge for us to function in our own individual callings from God, to connect with fellow warriors, and to properly discern our marching orders, so we can enlist, train and engage the enemy as part of an irresistible force. Read this book!"

—Bishop Eddie L. Long, senior pastor,
New Birth Missionary Baptist Church, Lithonia, Georgia

"Even the most gifted spiritual warriors need refreshment from time to time. *The Warrior's Heart* is a cool drink of water in the midst of battle. Whether you are a beginner or a veteran, with this book Harry Jackson will energize you for moving to a new level."

—C. Peter Wagner, chancellor, Wagner Leadership Institute,
Colorado Springs

"This is an outstanding book that will transform your community, your church and your life!"

—Che Ahn, senior pastor, Harvest Rock Church, Pasadena, California

"It's one thing to know how to have church, another to know how to live life. Bishop Jackson rescues Christianity from being merely a Sunday morning religious event and guides us into the abundant life of Christ. Spiritual warfare, to Bishop Jackson, is another phrase for 'living well.'"

—Francis Frangipane, founding pastor, River of Life Ministries,
Cedar Rapids, Iowa

"*The Warrior's Heart* is the most balanced book on spiritual warfare that I have ever read. It is practical, personal and spiritually powerful. I highly recommend this book."

—Judson Cornwall, pastor, teacher and author

"Harry Jackson is seeking to shake us awake—all who would serve, lead or take action as disciples of Jesus at this critical season of spiritual challenge. He's qualified as a faithful soldier; He's pointing the way as a servant-hearted leader."

—Jack Hayford, founding pastor, The Church On The Way, chancellor, The King's College and Seminary, Van Nuys, California

"This book may well challenge your concepts of spiritual warfare. Rather than a how-to manual of spiritual weaponry, Bishop Jackson's book is about warring from a place of solid, deep, inner strength. It's more about the warrior than the warfare. Delineating three specific and crucial areas—the warrior's inner life, the warrior's relationships and the warrior's corporate connections—Bishop Jackson makes a strong case for the importance of recognizing the source of our strength in combating the enemy: our relationships with God and others. It is well-written and contains practical applications as well as spiritual insights."

—Jane Hansen, president/CEO, Aglow International, Edmonds, Washington

"My friend Bishop Jackson writes with clarity and conviction. He guides us expertly through areas of godly living with personal as well as corporate connections. This book is a manual for effective believers today."

—John Bevere, author/speaker, John Bevere Ministries, Colorado Springs

"Bishop Harry Jackson has a heart that is gentle toward God and fierce against the enemy. He is an extremely gifted communicator who steps right into the ring to show us how to wage war against the power of Satan. Every believer needs this book."

—Cindy Jacobs, co-founder, Generals of Intercession, Colorado Springs

"With all the culture wars going on around us, if there's anything more needed in the Church today than a fighting spirit, I don't know what it is. Bishop Jackson's book *The Warrior's Heart* is not only a battle cry to every Christian to start contending for the faith in our time—to sign up, if you will—but it presents a clear, compelling and biblical roadmap to victory!"

—Bill McCartney, founder and president, Promise Keepers

THE
WARRIOR'S
HEART

*Rules of Engagement for the
Spiritual War Zone*

Harry R. Jackson Jr.

Chosen Books

A Division of Baker Book House Co
Grand Rapids, Michigan 49516

Published by Chosen Books
A division of Baker Book House Company
P.O. Box 6287, Grand Rapids, MI 49516-6287

Second printing, October 2004

Printed in the United States of America

Library of Congress Cataloging-in-Publication Data
Jackson, Harry R.
    The warrior's heart : rules of engagement for the spiritual war zone
/ Harry R. Jackson, Jr.
        p.   cm.
    Includes bibliographical references and index.
    ISBN 0-8007-9363-3 (pbk.)
    1. Spiritual warfare. I. Title
BV4509.5.J333 2004
235'.4—dc22   2003018204

Contents

Foreword

Much has been written in the last fifteen to twenty years on spiritual warfare. You will find very little, however, on the warrior himself. We humans are so often "cart before the horse" people. But the Bible is most definitely more about being than doing, becoming than accomplishing.

That is not to suggest a disinterest on God's part toward fruitful activity or the accomplishing of goals. He is very much a mission-minded God, so determined and confident of the outcome, in fact, that He dares to predict it in great detail. It's just that in this battle of good versus evil, darkness versus light, we who are a part of His overcoming battle strategy work primarily on the strength of who we are internally, not outwardly. In other words, victory is more about the warrior than the war. Therefore, the warrior's heart becomes the real issue as to whether we, at least for our sphere of the battle, win or lose!

Words like warfare, warrior and spiritual battle conjure up many images in the minds of Christians, and believe me, where it comes to this subject I've seen it all. Imbalances and extremes, over-emphases versus "I want no part of that stuff" mindsets are all realities and potential reactions. But fears of imbalance, fanaticism and casualties need not be a concern if we fight the good fight of faith from the proper perspective and *with a right heart*. And that is what this book is about.

This is not a book about screaming at demons or railing at the devil. It is not about warfare strategy—whether or not to march around our Jericho or run toward our giant. Rather, it is all about winning the war on the inside before we ever get to the giant or the stronghold. In short, it is making certain that no matter what our philosophy about spiritual warfare is, we overcome life's battles against the devil, whom all Bible-believing Christians know really exists. It's not about making you a *fighter*; it's about making you a *winner*.

I've known Harry Jackson for many years and watched him up close and from a distance. He is unique. I've met his wife and kids, his church staff and members. I tried to discern whether he was primarily intellectually driven or practically so, whether he was more of a worshiper or a warrior, a leader or a servant. I'm thrilled to tell you, because it isn't very common, that he is all of the above—a rare mix indeed.

Knowing the importance of his calling and ability, I told Harry a year or so ago, "You have been hidden as long as has been possible. From this time on, forget it—you have too much to say. 'The Lord hath need of thee.'" So here he comes, and right on time at that, to help take the Church to another level of overcoming. Thanks, Harry.

Sometimes it's okay to say, "I told you so."

Dutch Sheets

Acknowledgments

This book is lovingly dedicated to my mom, Essie Rountree Jackson, a powerful woman of prayer without whom I would not have been birthed into life or ministry. She is a woman with a warrior's heart.

It has been quite a journey getting this book to the public—six years in the making plus hours of prayer. There are so many people that I want to thank. First of all, the Lord Jesus Christ. Thank you, God, for the inspiration and the strength to complete this project.

Next, special thanks goes to my wife, Michele, who has encouraged me to press through all the hassles and get this book finished. This meant time away in writing and in prayer. Michele, you know what it means to have a warrior's heart. I also want to thank Elizabeth, my youngest daughter, who was so generous with her time during her last year in high school. Special thanks are also due to Joni Michele Jackson, my oldest daughter, biggest critic (on this book) and part-time proofreader and internal editor. You're going to be a writer yourself someday!

To my friends at Chosen/Baker Books, thanks for believing in me and the message of *The Warrior's Heart*. Jane Campbell, you have been an incredible source of encouragement—especially throughout the tedious polishing phase of the book. Thanks for the vision you had for this work.

To my editor, Jack Currie, your wisdom and insights were invaluable. Not only did you guide me through the arduous process of fine-tuning the "wordsmithing" of this project, you ultimately gave us the title. Thanks for your heart and attention to detail.

Walt Walker, you were the first to invest time in this book. Thank you for working through the original notes from my Bible school course. Like an experienced miner, you dug deep within the earth and eventually struck gold. You helped me see the true potential of the message.

Judson Cornwall, you were the first to say, "You've got something there!" The strength of that declaration has carried me far through the years of development it took to write this book. You know more than anyone that I placed this project on the altar many times before God made it live!

To Jan Sherman, staff researcher and internal editor for Christian Hope Ministries, thanks for minding the knitting. Your persistent attention to details has allowed this book to come to market despite building programs, incessant travel and the drama of local church life. You have had to live *The Warrior's Heart.* Hallelujah! We finally got it done.

Further thanks goes to Marcille Moss, Suren Adams, Joni Michele Jackson, Melissa Osborne and Renee Fox, who read every word of the manuscript over and over. Thank you all for resisting the temptation to rewrite the whole book!

Finally, the elders and deacons of Hope Christian Church along with the entire congregation deserve a round of applause. In fact, I am sure that the spiritual reward for this work will ultimately go to you. You have released me to write and travel. You have financed, supported and prayed an international ministry into existence. I love you all and am eternally indebted to you. You are the best.

Part 1

The Warrior's Inner Life

1

The Warrior's Heart

Love with an Attitude

Everything can be taken away from a man but one thing:
the last of the human freedoms—to choose one's attitude
in any given set of circumstances.[1]

Viktor Frankl

The flight from Washington, D.C., to Frankfurt gave me
a lot of time to think. I had never been to Germany and
was unsure how I would be received. In the long trans-
atlantic hours, I kept thinking about my dad's brother.
During World War II, Uncle Booker was a lieutenant in
the U.S. Army and part of the Allied occupying force in
Germany. My uncle served his country with honor and
distinction. Like so many G.I.s, he returned home, went
to college and started a career. He attended Tuskegee
Institute, which must have been his destiny. He was
named after its founder and most famous president,
Booker T. Washington.

The war had left its mark on my uncle. He saw a lot of horrible things that would come back to haunt him in recurring nightmares. Unlike some people, who do one significant thing and spend the balance of their lives talking about it, Uncle Booker never said too much about the war except when he would start drinking and eating Limburger cheese (which happened with some regularity).

As an African-American Army officer, he led a predominantly black platoon liberating prisoners from Nazi concentration camps. There he saw the extent to which Hitler's SS troops carried out his policies of Aryan-race supremacy. The sights, sounds and smells of those places were imprinted on his mind. Decades after the war he was still cursing Hitler for what he had done.

Hey, I thought, *that was over forty years ago. I shouldn't try to dig up issues that others dealt with so long ago.* With that, I turned my attention to the series of messages I was preparing to deliver at the Bible training school. How surprised I was to learn upon arriving that the school was located in a former SS compound! The facility still retained characteristics of its former use, including the original fortifications and gates. Taking a short walk into the woods, I discovered machine-gun bunkers spread across the hillside.

What an unlikely place for me to be! I had always been able to move easily among all kinds of ethnic groups. I grew up in an African-American neighborhood and attended a white private school. Guys from all kinds of backgrounds were best friends and teammates at Williams College. I went on to graduate training at Harvard Business School with students who represented an entirely different group of people. A person's background or the color of his skin has never been an issue for me. But speaking to a group of young Germans in an SS compound—well, if that does not make an

African-American self-conscious, there is nothing that ever would.

Wouldn't you know it, though—I cannot remember ever being more warmly received. That is what Christ does in people's hearts. I was told later that they had never sold more teaching tapes by a visiting teacher. The experience was good for me, especially after all that I had heard from Uncle Booker. I suppose that somewhere in the recesses of my mind, I was continuing to fight a war that had been over for more than forty years.

I had been working on becoming less of a fighter and more of a worshiper and a lover. The Bible is a book of love, and the very nature of God *is* love. So it seemed a little ironic when the dean of the school prayed for me and said, "Lord, give this man the heart of a warrior." It was a strange prayer, one that was almost funny, given the circumstances. But something about it resonated in my spirit, and God began to do a work in my heart.

The very next Sunday I was preaching in a large church on Long Island, New York. As I stood to address the congregation, I was immediately interrupted. A woman from the congregation jumped up, ran toward the front and ascended the platform. She began stuttering and stammering in an attempt to deliver a prophetic message. Not quite sure if this was considered normal in that church, I just froze. With the pastor out of town, the elders were looking at each other nervously, not knowing exactly what to do. So the woman continued until she finally got her message out: "I have given you the heart of a warrior."

At this point, God really had my attention. Before meeting Christ, I was a devoted athlete, playing college and professional football, wrestling and power-lifting. As a defensive lineman I had the reputation for making bone-crushing tackles, and my approach to competition was way over the edge. Since I had become a Christian, my primary focus had been to get rid of the warrior's heart. I had repented of it, renounced it and even had it cast out. As a Christian, following Christ meant putting away all the macho competitiveness to become a worshiper of God and a lover of people.

Ready: Wrestle

Now the Lord was clearly revealing another side to the Christian walk I had not seen yet. He was showing me that, even as we strive to demonstrate His love and advance His Kingdom, we are often at war—contending not with other people but with the spiritual forces of darkness. *So maybe there is a place for a warrior's heart, after all,* I concluded. This is what I would like to examine in this book.

Since my first trip to Germany fifteen years ago, I have learned many lessons about being a warrior for God. My personal warfare has been played out on three distinct fronts: inner battles, relational battles and corporate battles. Developing a warrior's heart is really a metaphor for becoming a high-impact Christian. Before I can achieve anything significant in life, I must make some firm decisions. It all starts with the heart.

Like everyone else who receives Christ, I wanted to learn of Him and make a difference for Him. My greatest challenge was to come to grips with the fact that things are never quite what they appear to be on the surface. The apostle Paul saw it this way:

> For our struggle is not against flesh and blood, but against the rulers, against the authorities, against the powers of this dark world and against the spiritual forces of evil in the heavenly realms.

> Ephesians 6:12

The battle against principalities and powers is not something you volunteer for. Every Christian is in one way or another involved in the unseen war. There are no bystanders, no spectators. It makes no difference how clearly you perceive the realities of the conflict or if you even believe in the existence of demonic spirits. Whether you participate as a combatant, a captive or an instrument of the enemy (even an unwitting instrument), be sure of this: You are in it, and the stakes are very high.

We must always keep in mind, though, that the battle is against the demonic forces of Satan—not against people who simply hold differing theological views. If we lose sight of this fundamental principle, we will spark conflicts with people that actually advance the enemy's goals rather than defeat them. Satan will always try to refocus our attention from the unseen and onto the seen, from the spiritual realm to the earthly. Keep the true enemy in your spiritual gun sights.

Understand that in discussing the realities of spiritual warfare I am not trying to oversimplify Christian discipleship or provide a formula to solve every human problem. Walking the Christian walk is not easy. Even so, it would be a grave mistake to miss the fact that our battle is against spiritual forces that are very real, though unseen.

Grasping the reality of the unseen war provides the foundation for victory over every bondage. We are called to live in the fullness of the Gospel for ourselves and take that fullness to the world in which we live. We are to affect our world. Each of us has a unique realm in which we have influence and authority. In that sphere God has called us to be salt and light. As Christians we have a biblical and moral mandate to make a difference. We must fight for personal victories while helping others as well.

Let's lift our vision higher, as the apostle Paul urges in 1 Corinthians 9:26, so that we will not be a community of faith that merely "beats the air." Beyond securing our homes, our families and our churches, let's change our society in the name of the Lord. This change will only occur as Christians view three things as strategic and make them available to God's higher purposes: (1) our unique circles of personal influence; (2) our positions in work and community service; and (3) our possessions.

Corresponding Realities in the Unseen World

Let me explain spiritual war this way. It is a battle between demonic forces and the forces of God in the earth. This battle originates in the unseen realm of the spirit but has consequences in the natural world. I would like to share a compelling observation from a man acquainted with the realities of war. The nineteenth-century military theorist Major-General Carl von Clausewitz said:

> War is nothing but a duel on a larger scale. Countless duels go to make up a war, but a picture of it as a whole can be formed by imagining a pair of wrestlers. Each tries through physical force to compel the other to do his will; his *immediate* aim is to *throw* his opponent in order to make him incapable of further resistance. *War is thus an act of force to compel our enemy to do our will.*[2]

This relationship between the seen and unseen worlds manifests itself in three ways:
The spiritual precedes the natural. Sometimes things happen on earth only because they are preceded by what has already happened in the heavenlies.

- Daniel fasted and prayed for more than twenty days for the Lord to come to his aid. Finally an angel appeared to him, saying that he had been delayed because he was warring with a demonic principality that had resisted him (see Daniel 10:12–13).
- In John the apostle's revelation, events on earth took place as a result of the seals on the heavenly scroll being broken (see Revelation 5–6).

The natural explains the spiritual. God also uses the natural realm as a way to explain unseen realities. Things in the natural serve as models of things in the spiritual. The exodus from Egypt, for example, was a natural event that reflected the work of salvation, baptism and deliverance from bondage. The tabernacle on earth was a replica of the temple in heaven.

The natural precedes the spiritual. Other times, natural events precede spiritual events. They are like prophetic foreshadows of spiritual things to come. The apostle Paul wrote to the Corinthian church, "The spiritual did not come first, but the natural, and after that the spiritual" (1 Corinthians 15:46). The apostle was referring to the first Adam—a natural man and a prophetic foreshadowing of Christ. The first Adam gave us physical life, and the last Adam (Christ) gave us spiritual life. The natural came first as a prophetic signpost, then the spiritual.

Multi-Level Revolution

Things that are happening in the natural world give us insight into what is happening in the spirit realm. In the last few years, we have witnessed one atrocity after another as age-old ethnic rivalries have erupted. Rwanda, Somalia, Bosnia and Kosovo are just a few of the names with which we have all become familiar. After 9/11, Afghanistan and the war on Iraq, no one can ignore the centuries-long conflict between Islam and Christianity. This struggle goes back to the days of the Crusades. It continues to reemerge in the most unlikely locations. There are scores of other regional conflicts waiting to boil over into all-out war. Since the collapse of the Soviet Union, political affiliations and geographic boundaries all over the world have been changing so fast that maps are going out of date as fast as they can be redrawn.

Can we attribute this soley to political and social causes? Not if we consider the apostle Paul's words to the philosophers on Mars Hill: "From one man he made every nation of men, that they should inhabit the whole earth; and he determined the times set for them and the exact places where they should live" (Acts 17:26). Political structures and boundaries change because something in the spiritual realm changed first.

Most of the regional wars are the result of ethnic conflicts that are hundreds of years old. Thousands are being massacred in what amounts to tribal warfare. We created a horrible new word to describe the atrocities that took place in southern Europe: ethnic cleansing. It is hard for those outside these regions to understand the power of bitterness and resentment. It creates in people a fanatical spirit, so driven by a passion for revenge that there is no moral restraint against committing atrocities.

In light of international events, I believe God wants us to understand that there is a tremendous need for the Church to restructure, reorganize and realign its priorities in order to become more relevant to the needs of individual people. I also believe that just as God is realigning the boundaries and affiliations in the political world, He is challenging the Church to deal with her own repressed tensions, divisions and ethnic tribalism.

How are we to view all this geopolitical turmoil? What do these events mean to us as individual Christians, as the Church, as well as to us as a nation? It is important to understand that there are four realms of God-ordained authority in the earth: the individual, who is responsible to govern himself under God; the family; the Church; and the civil government. The Bible says, "The authorities that exist have been established by God" (Romans 13:1). Consequently, when the King of kings and Lord of lords has something to say, it relates to each and all spheres of authority. When you see such evidence that God is "appointing" and "determining" things regarding global affairs on earth, you can be sure that it has implications for other realms of authority. What we see in the natural world, that is, the realignment of geopolitical forces, becomes a prophetic foreshadowing of what God intends to do in other realms of authority—in our homes, personal lives and churches.

To the extent that conflict-resolution methods are biblical, we need to employ them on all levels to bring peace in the family, the Church and the nations. At the same time, there is no way to understand these events apart from unseen spiritual warfare. John Dawson, author of *Taking Our Cities for God* and *Healing America's Wounds*,[3] explains that spiritual strongholds are built upon offenses and bitterness that have developed among social, ethnic and economic groups.

We live in a fallen world full of humans whose natures have been infected with sin. Were it not for God's restraining grace, the human race would have destroyed itself long ago. God, in the wisdom of His plan, has seen fit to withdraw His restraining hand to allow ethnic tensions all over the world to boil over into a multitude of conflicts.

When you see these things happening, do not be surprised when the Holy Spirit begins to point out corresponding, unresolved issues in the Body of Christ. Recognize the hand of God and remember that He is allowing them to surface because He wants to deal with them. If we respond to the authority of the Holy Spirit and realign ourselves with what He is trying to accomplish, we will find a new measure of grace, a greater outward manifestation of His presence and a clearer sense of His purpose.

The nations are coming apart, dividing up into little ethnic fiefdoms led by men who perpetuate age-old prejudice and motivate people by reminding them of offenses from years gone by. The Church is the only institution that can change this trend. God has ordained that believers in Christ become a new ethnic group. This is clearly the teaching of the apostle Peter (see 1 Peter 2:9) and the apostle Paul (see Ephesians 2:14–19). As leaders and as believers, we need to be reconciled, to forgive and to be one in Christ.

Just as there is chaos in the sphere of governmental authority, the authority structures in the home are crumbling. I believe households are also in need of reordering and restructuring. It is predicted that 70 percent of black households will be without a male authority figure by the year 2007. Can the deterioration of these families be understood as spiritual warfare? You bet it can.

God has a great concern for the children of the next generation. His desire is to raise them up in His image. Satan tried to destroy the Messiah, his adversary, when he prompted King Herod to slaughter the children of Bethlehem. In the same way, Satan seeks to destroy the family structure. With the authority figure removed, he proceeds to enslave an entire generation all over again. This is spiritual war. General George S. Patton said:

Every single man in this Army plays a vital role. Don't ever let up. Don't ever think that your job is unimportant. Every man has a job to do and he must do it. Every man is a vital link in the great chain.[4]

If you take Patton's advice to heart, the remainder of this book will help you (1) find your place in the Son, (2) recognize and connect to significant relationships and (3) embrace and move in the corporate anointing of the ministry team to which you have been assigned. As you read the pages of this book, my prayer is that you will enlist, train and engage in war, and that you will find your own warrior's heart.

2

Honor Code and Conscience

Hearing the Voice of God

> Every conscience needs instruction. Its delicate mechanism has been thrown off balance by the Fall. Just as a bullet will reach the bull's eye only if the two sights are in correct alignment, so correct moral judgments are delivered only when the conscience is correctly aligned with the Scriptures.[1]
>
> J. Oswald Sanders

Most of us remember January 17, 1991, the night Operation Desert Storm began. We sat in front of our television sets and watched the skies over Baghdad light up with tracer bullets from hundreds of antiaircraft guns firing wildly into the night. In the following days we were amazed to see replays of laser-guided smart bombs being directed right into the front door of a building. Aspects of that campaign parallel what we deal with every day in spiritual warfare. For example, in the first days of the attack, the primary objective was to take out radar sites and all command-and-control capabilities. The strategy was to blind the enemy and cut off communications between frontline forces and their commanders.

We fight against similar tactics, against principalities and powers of darkness that desire to cut the lines of communication with our Commander. Staying in contact with our heavenly chain of command is essential for personal and corporate victory in the unseen war.

In a very hands-on way, this chapter will address how to receive guidance from God. There are many books written on this topic, but they often underestimate the role of the human conscience.

Let me compare navigating our lives to driving a car. In a car we need a gas gauge, an odometer, an engine temperature gauge and many other helpful devices that monitor the smooth operation of the vehicle. Similarly, in navigating our personal lives, we need: (1) the Word of God; (2) the Holy Spirit; (3) circumstances; and (4) our consciences. As Donald Grey Barnhouse wrote, "The conscience may be likened to a sundial that is made for the sun, even as the conscience rightly directed, reflects God's will."[2]

Haven't we all heard strange things described as the guidance of the Lord? Truth is often stranger than fiction. David Koresh built an armed compound and defended his rights in the name of the Lord. Mothers have beaten their children to death to exorcise demons. Parents have withheld life-sustaining medicine from their kids. Others have divorced their spouses, left their jobs or split a thriving church in response to a still, small voice or Scripture. This "guidance" later proved to be anything *but* the voice of God.

A few years ago I had the opportunity to host a national ministry event in our city. As I sat and meditated on a course of action, the thought popped into my mind that if I did not take on this responsibility and the considerable expenses attached to it, one of the other churches in the city would literally jump at the chance. It was then that I felt "led" to host the event.

Unfortunately for both my church and myself, the event was an expensive flop. My competitive nature, a touch of unforgiveness and opportunism pushed me into a big mistake. My state of mind had temporarily put my conscience on pause. Most of us could cite moments in which we became temporarily "confused" and mistook our own misguided agendas for the will of God.

What Matters Besides Sincerity?

A clear and clean conscience is a safe guide. If your conscience is damaged or defiled, however, you can diligently follow the voice of your conscience and not be following God.

One night at worship-team rehearsal we were dealing with some issues about how we should worship. Someone made the comment that if we just worshiped from our hearts, wouldn't everything be fine? I had to gracefully disagree.

Simply being led by our hearts is only as safe as the conditions of our hearts. Jeremiah 17:9 says, "The heart is deceitful above all things and beyond cure. Who can understand it?" So let's not be confused and say, "As long as it's from my heart, it's okay." That sounds like the sad commentary on the state of Israel in the last verse of the book of Judges: "In those days Israel had no king; everyone did as he saw fit" (Judges 21:25).

God has a standard; He has a pattern. Our job is to conform to His pattern, not to have Him lower His standards to our level. Worship, you see, has a warfare aspect to it. When we worship, the Church pulls down strongholds as surely as those who went out before Jehoshaphat's army singing praises, thus defeating the Ammonites and Moabites (see 2 Chronicles 20). If spiritual warfare was not such an important aspect of the Christian life, I suppose it would be easier to accept the nothing-matters-but-sincerity approach. That is the way it usually works in a family setting—it is the thought that counts. But it is not so in warfare. What matters is obeying orders. Acceptable worship, Jesus said, must be offered in "spirit and *truth*," not just with good motives.

All of us have experienced worship services in which some people were blessed and others were not. Although we all claim the guidance of the Spirit, there are moments when we truly sense the manifest presence of God and that the heart of God is pleased. Everyone in the service knows it. My discussion with my worship team was designed to bring them to a place where they could separate their own preferences from the guidance of the Holy Spirit.

The first step to making the conscience an accurate communications and navigational instrument is to dispel all humanistic ideas that equate sincerity of heart with God's will. We can be sincerely misdirected when we follow our own desires because God's calling sometimes leads us in the very opposite direction. The Holy Spirit guides us most clearly when our consciences have learned to distinguish between our sincere desires and the moral code of the Word of God. Our consciences screen out actions and directions that would violate the Word of God and the character of God. Our consciences are meant to be screening devices that tell us which things are "off limits." Our consciences are like the virus screening software used in a computer. These programs identify and destroy things that would hinder or defile the normal operation of our programming.

Going for the Hidden Stuff

God uses our consciences to shed light on our motives, thoughts and actions. Proverbs 20:27 says, "The lamp of the LORD searches the spirit of a man; it searches out his inmost being." The purpose of the Holy Spirit in the lives of believers is to conform them to the image of Christ. For the fruit of the Spirit to be evident, there are usually a lot of dark closets that need to be cleaned out. The innermost closets are the ones where we hide our secrets, things we do not want others to know about and things we do not want to think about ourselves. Have you ever noticed how the Holy Spirit will skip over all of the things you want to talk about and go straight for the hidden stuff?

When we come to God in prayer, certain things will rise up in our spirits. If we do not deal with the persuasive voice of the Holy Spirit, we may begin to feel separated from God. Many times a sense of emotional pressure accompanies this feeling of distance from God. Isaiah 59:2 says, "But your iniquities have separated you from your God; your sins have hidden his face from you, so that he will not hear." Repentance can easily remove the sense of distance. Repent about what? Perhaps God is dealing with the motives, habits or actions with which we have become accustomed. When the Holy Spirit begins to bring things to your mind, therefore, deal with those thoughts. Do not keep squashing them down; do not keep trying to change the subject. God wants to deal with those areas in your prayer time.

Interpreting the Voices

"Picking your hill to die upon" is an expression that means *figure out what it is that is important enough to defend with your life.* We must pay the spiritual price to stay connected with God! *This* is your hill. To cultivate your ability to discern between condemnation of the devil and conviction of the Holy Spirit, you have to fight the fight of faith, becoming firmly convinced that God loves you and accepts you, that He corrects His children because He loves them. In our spiritual war, we must contend for communion with God. Both your own flesh and satanic mind games attempt to hinder you in establishing this closeness with God.

Recognizing the voice of God becomes much easier if we examine a few things. There are many books that explain how to hear the voice of God. What is often missing is an explanation of the role and function of your conscience. First of all, you have to discern where the thoughts are coming from. Is it the accusing voice of the enemy condemning you or is it really the Holy Spirit? Next, if there have been deep wounds in your life in some areas, it is not easy to discern the conviction of the Spirit. Those who have struggled with rejection are especially prone to feel that any thought of sin that arises means they are condemned and rejected by God. They either give up on prayer or learn to repress any such feelings.

Most managers have had the experience of trying to train an employee who interprets all correction and instruction as a statement of his self-worth and job security—or the lack thereof. It is easy to get frustrated with such a relationship. In a spiritual sense, you can imagine how Satan, the accuser of the brethren, can have a field day with such a person. After all the psychological concepts have been shared and shared again, it comes down to spiritual warfare. We simply have to take a position and defend it. With the helmet of salvation protecting our thought lives and the shield of faith firmly in hand, we have a defense against Satan's flaming missiles.

Twofold Assurance

Faith in God easily flows out of a heart that is basking in the inner peace of God. In the absence of inner turmoil, we have an almost automatic confidence in the power and presence of God working on our behalf. We have an assurance that our Champion and Commander in Chief, Jesus, can defeat every enemy in our lives. There seem to be two factors that contribute to this kind of assurance: (1) Our own hearts assure us, "This then is how we know that we belong to the truth, and how we set our hearts at rest in his presence" (1 John 3:19), and (2) The Holy Spirit within us, "whenever our hearts condemn us. For God is greater than our hearts, and he knows everything" (1 John 3:20). A clear conscience is the result of God's Spirit and our own hearts both bearing witness together. This is the same thing Paul referred to when he wrote: "Therefore, there is now no condemnation for those who are in Christ Jesus. . . . The Spirit himself testifies with our spirit that we are God's children" (Romans 8:1, 16).

The first step in the process of learning to be led by the Holy Spirit is learning to distinguish between condemnation of the devil and conviction of the Holy Spirit. This kind of discernment is critical for spiritual health. Cultivating an understanding about God's guidance will ultimately be one of the most important spiritual assets we can possess. In a sense, this kind of discernment can seem defensive, but as warriors whose mission is to advance the Kingdom of God, we cannot just defend our position. We also have to go on the offensive. That means instant obedience—stepping out in faith to obey the impressions of the Spirit. We should cultivate an ability to discern His leading and practice the habit of instant and complete obedience.

Commanded by Conscience

It is a 25-minute drive from my house to the U.S. Naval Academy in Annapolis, Maryland. Naval midshipmen, as well as the cadets from the other service academies, are required to live by an honor code. It is made plain to all new cadets that the code is not something they are to pick up by the second, third or fourth year; it is the very basis and starting point of all their military training. Honesty, integrity and trust are essential to any military organization. A person who will lie, cheat or steal in a small thing, is as likely—if not more likely—to do so in a weighty matter. In time of war, soldiers must be able to entrust their lives to one another in the most difficult and stressful situations. As Sterne wrote in *Tristram Shandy,* "Trust that man in nothing; who has not a conscience in everything."[3]

One way that Christians are to be soldiers is by guarding their consciences as the most prized of their possessions. James Madison once wrote, "Conscience is the most sacred of all property."[4]

The word *conscience* is not found at all in the Old Testament. The closest reference is in Proverbs 20:27: "The lamp of the LORD searches the spirit of a man; it searches out his inmost being." In the New Testament, there are thirty references to the Greek word *suneidesis,* which is translated "conscience." Spiros Zodhiates, a highly respected Greek scholar and executive editor of *Hebrew-Greek Key Word Study Bibles,* says, "It denotes an abiding conscious-

31

ness whose nature it is to bear inner witness to one's own conduct in a moral sense. It is self-awareness."[5]

The English word *conscience* is derived from the word *conscientia,* which means three things. First of all, it is the knowledge within; second, it is the moral realm; and third, it is a recognition or distinguishing between good and evil.

Everyone's inner life is different. The New Testament writers talk about those who have a good conscience (see Acts 23:1; 1 Timothy 1:5, 19; Hebrews 13:18; 1 Peter 3:16, 21), a pure conscience (see 1 Timothy 3:9; 2 Timothy 1:3), a conscience void of offense (see Acts 24:16) and a conscience that has been purged from the consciousness of sin. They also describe what happens to the consciences of those who have developed the habit of ignoring this inner voice. When a person forges ahead after his own lust or retreats from acknowledging the truth, his conscience is weakened.

Components of Conscience

All men and women alike have a conscience, but its condition and influence on their words and deeds varies greatly from person to person. For many, the conscience is simply the basis for regret and afterthought. Others are actually prevented from action by the powerful influence of their consciences. Interestingly, our consciences can be developed or damaged. So let's look at some of the factors that shape our consciences.

The Image of God in Us

You do not have to be a Christian or even a believer in God to have a conscience. It is something put into each person because each is made in the image of God. It is the rule of God imparted to every man and woman. In fact, those who have never had the opportunity to hear the Gospel of Jesus Christ will in the end be judged by how they have responded to their own consciences.

> (Indeed, when Gentiles, who do not have the law, do by nature things required by the law, they are a law for themselves, even though they do not have the law, since they show that the requirements of the law are written on their hearts, their consciences also bearing witness, and their thoughts now accusing, now even defending them.) This will take place on the day when God will judge men's secrets through Jesus Christ, as my gospel declares.
>
> Romans 2:14–16

According to Paul, judgment will be rendered to unknowing pagans according to what they did with their consciences: whether they acknowledged the moral truth revealed to them or suppressed that self-evident truth in unrighteousness (see Romans 1:18); whether they repented because of their consciences' rebukes or forged ahead into sin. Historically, those who have rejected the self-evident truth about God were given over to depraved minds, to degrading passions and fell away from God (see Romans 1:24, 26, 28). This is the process through which false religions were birthed after Adam and Eve's fall. In the succeeding verses Paul repeats three times the phrase *God gave them over* (to greater degrees of sin). Because they pridefully rejected the convictions of their consciences, the grace of God that restrained them was removed.

The Influence of the Surrounding Culture

In his letter to Titus, Paul seems to be saying that the culture in which we are raised affects our consciences.

Even one of their own prophets has said, "Cretans are always liars, evil brutes, lazy gluttons." This testimony is true. Therefore, rebuke them sharply, so that they will be sound in the faith and will pay no attention to Jewish myths or to the commands of those who reject the truth. To the pure, all things are pure, but to those who are corrupted and do not believe, nothing is pure. In fact, both their minds and consciences are corrupted.

Titus 1:12–15

That is a powerful statement, especially when you consider the fact that Paul is referring in this passage to believers. In a fallen culture, people often think they are doing well when they are actually falling far shorter than they realize. Because American society is so sex-crazed, many single people who stop just short of actual intercourse consider themselves to have high moral standards. They say, like a well-known political figure who was caught in a compromising situation, "I did not have sex with that woman." Seeing so much sex, violence and profanity in the media desensitizes our consciences to the extent that we are no longer convicted and appalled by murder, pornography or a dire lack of integrity. It is important for us to remember that the Word of God is our standard, not movies, television sitcoms or what is acceptable to the majority of those around us.

Living in a debased culture also affects the Church as a whole. In certain kinds of churches there are particular sins that have come to be acceptable. I know personally of one congregation in which the pastor has a girlfriend sitting in the front row on one side of the church and his wife sitting on the other side. How ridiculous that is! It is a known situation, yet everything proceeds as if that were normal. Why isn't something done about it? In this case, it is an issue of the conscience of an entire congregation being defiled. In the context of the world we live in, they have decided that this kind of sin is tolerable. The problem is that God judges us by the context of His Word, not our surroundings.

In societies where there has been an unrelenting march downward from integrity and conscience, Satan always overplays his hand. Eventually, people get so sick of the corruption of their culture and of their own lives, they begin to hunger and thirst for righteousness again. The good news is that when you live in such darkness, it does not take much to be a bright light. Just acting like a normal Christian is an extremely radical thing to do.

Shaped by Training and Upbringing

In recent years, as I have interviewed prospective church employees, I have gotten into the habit of asking questions about their home lives; I explore some foundational relationships. I ask people how they related to their fathers and mothers, teachers, coaches and pastors. I ask questions and listen very carefully, not just to what they say, but what comes through the spirit of each person.

Our consciences are derived in large measure from what we were taught by our parents and grandparents. When we hire people at the church, I expect them to have a warrior's heart that is founded in integrity—like that of a good and well-trained soldier. I ask questions, searching for evidence of an honor code with a high standard. I probe for what their parents imparted to them and if, after all these years, it is still there. With a little practice, it is not hard to tell if there is a malfunction in someone's conscience.

And it is definitely possible for someone's conscience to malfunction. Titus 1:15 would call this kind of malfunction a "corruption." The Greek word used here is *miaino,* which means literally "to dye with another color or stain." This is a great illustration of how our consciences are defiled. In the ancient world one could change the color of a cloth only by dipping it repeatedly into a dye pot. The depth of the color was determined by how many times the cloth was dipped. This is the same way our consciences are changed from their original color. Those who have not dealt thoroughly with an earlier habit of violating their consciences have a discernible stain on their spirits. Stains of sin can indeed be washed clean by the blood but not without serious repentance and rededication.

I have talked to some potential employees who have come from horrible situations. God, however, had done a wonderful healing work in them and there was no trace of the past in their spirits. The best way I can think to illustrate what I mean is the example of the three Hebrews who were thrown into the furnace of fire by King Nebuchadnezzar. Their names were Shadrach, Meshach and Abednego. The Scriptures say that after they were delivered from the fire, these young men did not even have the smell of smoke on them. Many of my most productive and valued employees have been delivered from their pasts as completely as the three Hebrew boys. Their consciences have been cleansed and the past hurts are healed. That is how I think of these people, as those who have been delivered from the fire without even the smell of smoke left on them.

Our Own Personal Convictions

The apostle Paul wrote to the Corinthian church that had a lot of problems, one of which had to do with eating meat sacrificed to idols. To eat such meat was strictly forbidden by the law of Moses. Reading 1 Corinthians 8 you get the clear impression that Paul understood that Christians were free from that particular ceremonial law. Nevertheless, there were those who could not eat without violating their consciences. Note this interesting point: Even though Paul did not think there was anything wrong with eating the meat, he also said that eating meat against the dictates of one's own conscience would cause it to be defiled (see 1 Corinthians 8:7). Not only that, those who encourage others to "take their liberty" against the dictates of their consciences sin in two ways: (1) "When you sin against your brothers in this way and wound their weak conscience, (2) you sin against Christ" (1 Corinthians 8:12). What other statement can show more clearly how important it is to cultivate and protect the inward register of one's conscience!

The Accusation of the Evil One

It is not uncommon for people to spend the balance of their lives agonizing over sins and mistakes of the past. I have already discussed this problem a little, but it is important to realize that the foundation of a person's conscience may be influenced by an unscriptural sense of guilt before God. When we put the whole of our faith in Jesus Christ as Savior and Lord, He forgives us for all that we have done and begins the process of changing who we are. Because of the blood of Jesus, we can stand before God with a clean conscience. The writer of Hebrews states, "Let us draw near to God with a sincere heart in full assurance of faith, having our hearts sprinkled to cleanse us from a guilty conscience and having our bodies washed with pure water" (Hebrews 10:22).

Being assured of how we stand before God is a matter of spiritual warfare. Satan is described in John's Revelation this way: "For the accuser of our brothers, who accuses them before our God day and night, has been hurled down" (Revelation 12:10). It is for this reason that part of the armor of God Paul talks about is designed for protection against accusation. "In addition to all this, take up the shield of faith, with which you can extinguish all the flaming arrows of the evil one" (Ephesians 6:16). A clean and clear conscience is the result of forgiveness bought by Christ's blood and a consistent daily lifestyle of integrity.

A Cultivated Sensitivity

When you make a habit of listening to your conscience, you become more and more sensitive to its voice. Abraham Lincoln was a man who considered his honor and integrity as his most valuable possessions. Even in his own time he was called "Honest Abe." Men and women, whose ethical nerve endings have lost their sensitivity, regularly stumble into fraudulent promises, conflicts of interest and misleading statements. Most of the time they are not aware of it. In contrast, Abraham Lincoln was at all times sensitive to his own personal honor and to anything that might tarnish it.

One of the stories of Lincoln's sensitivity to compromising situations goes like this: All clients knew that, with Old Abe as their lawyer, they would win their cases—if Abe believed in their cause. If a case was not fair, then it was a waste of time to take it to him. One day, after listening for some time to a would-be client's statement, with his eyes staring at the ceiling, Lincoln swung around in his chair and exclaimed:

> Well, you have a pretty good case in technical law but a pretty bad one in equity and justice. You'll have to get some other fellow to win this case for you. I couldn't do it. All the time while standing talking to that jury I'd be thinking, "Lincoln, you're a liar," and I believe I should forget myself and say it out loud.[6]

In other words, Lincoln was concerned that his conscience would prompt him to speak out against his client in public. He, therefore, never took an unworthy case. Compared to the legal dream teams of our day, he lacked the killer instinct to be a trial lawyer. Perhaps Lincoln was actually trying his cases before a "higher court."

Every time you or I ignore the inner moral voice, by whatever rationalization we justify the decision, we defile our consciences. And each time this happens, it becomes a little easier. The inner convictions are a little weaker; the inner voice speaks to us a little softer. Before long, we are able to commit sin without a tinge of conviction. If we continue defiling the conscience each step of the way, we will go into deeper and darker practices. If we do not stop this cycle by repentance, we will eventually end up as reprobates with no discernible conscience at all.

"But solid food is for the mature," says Hebrews 5:14, "who by constant use have trained themselves to distinguish good from evil." A righteous man or woman diligently guards his or her heart as to a good soldier guards the most strategic of all positions. In time, he or she will develop an acute and discerning sensitivity to the inner conscience.

Fine-Tuning Our Consciences to the Will of God

Years of living with oneself as lord can leave one's conscience in great need of renewal. Suppressing and defiling the conscience can leave it seared and insensitive to some really egregious kinds of sin. This is not unlike the Gentiles in Paul's churches who formerly participated in pagan cults. Sin was practiced in those places as if it were a virtuous act. In such cases, your conscience can become insensitive and "hard of hearing" to the voice of the Spirit.

On the other hand, hurts, fears and lack of faith in the Word of God can cause you to be far too sensitive in some areas. In extreme cases, people make every action of life an issue of conscience. You might say they have a "hyperactive conscience," causing them to take absolute, uncompromising positions on relatively inconsequential matters. They might feel, for example, "as a matter of conscience," that all Scripture should be read from a particular translation and only with the congregation standing. As ridiculous as this may sound, many believers have drawn lines in the sand that separate them from the broader Body of Christ. Obviously this hurts the unity of the Church. More practically it isolates needy people from the friendships and connections that they need to fulfill their unique callings on the earth. As a result of their inability to discern between preference, conscience and the voice of the Spirit, they become intolerant legalists. They may also be concentrating on minor points as a way of compensating for a major sin that has never been dealt with.

What we want to do is readjust our consciences so that they are in harmony with the divinely ordained registry, so that they witness to right or wrong according to what God thinks and feels. There are three ways this is accomplished.

By Reproof and Correction

We have to learn to receive correction from trusted spiritual leaders. Just as children must respond to the intense training of loving parents, we must learn that God uses strategic relationships to shape us. These relationships are most typically with local church leaders. Our peers often have the same blind spots that we do.

We must, therefore, seek out and respond to our chosen mentors and disciplers. This concept is very biblical.

Remember Paul's assessment of the Cretans that I mentioned earlier in this chapter. Because of their cultural background, the Cretans had problems to which they were not very sensitive. They tolerated lying, laziness and gluttony. Paul's scriptural remedy for these kinds of problems was very simple. "Therefore, rebuke them sharply, so that they will be sound in the faith and will pay no attention to Jewish myths or to the commands of those who reject the truth" (Titus 1:13).

A "sharp rebuke" says that this particular sin will not be tolerated. Harlem does not have the same kinds of problems that Hollywood has. There will be different issues in every cultural setting. Christian leaders need to articulate a sharp, biblically based rebuke for sin wherever it is detected. Paul said (in the common vernacular of today), "Some folks' consciences just don't work. Therefore, set the standard by rebuking them sharply."

By Sincere Repentance

Repentance may seem like too simple a prescription for the problems outlined in this chapter. But it is very important that we embrace a lifestyle of repentance. As we walk in the power of the love of Christ and the reality of the new birth, our consciences are recalibrated.

G. Campbell Morgan, one of the twentieth century's finest expository preachers, identified the connection between conscience and truth when he wrote:

Conscience is that thing which calls things by their right name, refuses to allow any evil thing to be baptized by a name that robs it of its real meaning and significance. Conscience will call a lie a lie, and will not allow a man to escape by applying to it the high sounding name of hyperbole. Conscience cannot prevent a man saying the untrue thing, but it will trouble him. . . . It is always unveiling the truth, always unmasking a lie, forever warning the soul against the wrong of wrong and the peril of wrong.[7]

Repentance of all known sin is necessary if you and I are going to readjust our consciences. The apostle John wrote:

If we claim to have fellowship with him yet walk in the darkness, we lie and do not live by the truth. But if we walk in the light, as he is in the light, we have fellowship with one another, and the blood of Jesus, his Son, purifies us from all sin. If we claim to be without sin, we deceive ourselves and the truth is not in us.

1 John 1:6–8

When questioned by a superior officer, there are only four answers available to new West Point cadets. They are "Yes, sir," "No, sir," "I do not understand, sir" and "No excuse, sir." When asked why a duty or an order was not carried out to an acceptable standard, it makes no difference whether or not there were valid excuses. That answer is not an option. Yes, no or no excuse—sir. There is a reason for this kind of military training. They are molding leaders who do not make excuses or blame others, but rather accept personal responsibility. How different that is from the common and well-refined art of evading the uncomfortable truth by blame-shifting!

The issue here is denial—categorizing personal sin in a way that shifts personal blame and responsibility to others. Call it codependency or any other psychological term, but for true repentance to take place, genuine confession must precede it. John continues in the next verse, "If we confess our sins, he is faithful and just and will forgive us our sins and purify us from all unrighteousness" (1 John 1:9).

Covering our sins will produce progressive darkness. Matthew 6:23 says, "But if your eyes are bad, your whole body will be full of darkness. If then the light within you is darkness, how great is that darkness!" God sees the twistedness in our nature that tries to hide from the truth. But when we respond to the convicting power of the Holy Spirit and humble ourselves and acknowledge the truth, God gives us grace to appropriate all the transforming power of the cross.

It seems to be the flip side of God's judgment. Romans 1:28 says that from those who refuse to acknowledge self-evident truth, God removes His restraining grace and gives them over to depravity. Conversely, to those who humble themselves and acknowledge the conviction of the Holy Spirit, God gives greater grace. James 4:6 says, "But he gives us more grace. That is why Scripture says: 'God opposes the proud but gives grace to the humble.'"

Sinners are those who sin by habit and sin by practice. They practice sin and, consequently, they get better at it. Saints are those who, by practice, do the right thing but who occasionally sin. Thank God He is going to allow us to receive forgiveness for the sins we do commit and change the areas that are undisciplined and unruly before God.

By Faith in the Blood of Jesus

The inward cleansing of the blood of Jesus at salvation is supposed to free us and bring us to a place where our consciences can immediately work appropriately. At the outset of the new birth, there is a spiritual work of erasing our sins that takes place in the spiritual realm. In other words, heaven's courts will not hold us responsible for past sins. This should produce a sense of joy in our lives and confidence as we pray. All too often, what happens is the voice of our consciences malfunctions because we focus upon tradition and societal pressures despite the new sensitivity we feel on the inside. Consequently we do not necessarily take full advantage of the provision of salvation after we are born again.

Conclusion

The problem with divine guidance is that it is often one step at a time. Further, the Lord delights to communicate with us on His own terms. It is surprising for many believers that much of the Lord's significant direction for our lives is nonverbal. God seems to be of the same mindset as our state highway departments. He boldly erects signs, signals and symbols, expecting us to read the driver's manual and act accordingly. No one foolishly waits at a green light until he or she can remember a line from the manual. Conversely, no voice from heaven will speak a warning as we barrel past a stop sign.

Let's not get hung up on the methods of God's guidance. Let's determine to pursue His individual calling for our lives. As we seek to unravel the mystery of His will (see Ephesians 1:9), our consciences will play a big part in the process.

Remember that there is a unique assignment on your life. We have been chosen by God, each one of us for a special purpose. As farfetched as it may sound, you can become an integral part of God's plan in this generation. Whether you are 19, 39, 59 or older, God can use anyone who tunes his or her heart and conscience to His voice. Ordinary people can do extraordinary works as they follow the guidance of God.

3

The Warrior's Inner Strength

Gateway to Joy

> When we do the best that we can, we never know what
> miracle is wrought in our life, or in the life of another.
>
> Helen Keller

I will never forget that Sunday. It was one of the worst
days of my life. I knelt before the altar feeling numb
inside. The thoughts kept running through my mind,
You're in trouble. You'll never get out of this. I hadn't slept
much the night before because my mind kept going back
to the huge tax debt that my church owed the IRS.

The bad news arrived the previous Friday. The agent
had been relatively kind but told me that I could be
held personally responsible for unpaid payroll taxes. I
assured this clean-shaven representative of the federal
government that there must be some mistake. Just as
soon as my staff came in that morning, I would be able

to clear everything up. I promised the agent a prompt response by early the next week.

The awful truth came out late Friday, after an amazing time of corporate prayer. We found that the taxes had indeed gone unpaid for more than a year. Without trying to affix any blame, I would like to note that this little "business decision" had been kept from me, and the other church leaders as well. We owed $250,000, a lot of money, particularly in light of the remodeling process underway at the church.

Where would we get the money? Should I resign? Should I take legal action? Aside from all of this, I was totally unable to connect with God in worship. The greatest thing about Sunday for me is the opportunity to worship the Lord. I always relish the time spent in both singing and prayer. This Sunday, however, was very different.

Looking at the floor, I heard the still, small voice say, *Your problem is that you are trying to win!* I suddenly understood a great deal. This battle was *not* just about me. I could not tackle anybody or lash out at a foe. This was a Kingdom thing. God was going to have to lead me.

Just as I was agonizing over this information, I heard the guest speaker address our congregation, declaring, "This church is going through the greatest trial of its history, but in the end, the Lord will be glorified."

I was so encouraged by this amazing word that I was strengthened through the entire year that it took to pay off the IRS. What a wonderful gift prophecy can be when used correctly! Yet the greatest gift that I received during that period was *not* prophecy. It was joy. Inward joy gave me the strength to overcome fear and carry on.

Modern soldiers go through rigorous physical training, not only as a means of discipline and self-mastery, but also as preparation for actual battle. There are a lot of physical demands placed upon soldiers in times of war. Technology can make up for human limitations in a great number of modern military conflicts. And, of course, it does not take a lot of strength to pull a trigger or push the button on a missile launcher. A kid in the mountains of Bosnia or in the rice paddies of Vietnam can do that, but physical prowess is still needed. When the Bible speaks of the followers of Christ as soldiers, it is in the context of ancient warfare. In biblical times warfare was almost completely hand-to-hand combat. In a battle with weapons of that period, victory was determined for the most part by skill, strength and endurance.

It is difficult for most of us to imagine a combat situation in which your life hangs in the balance, where people previously working as farmers, bankers and teachers become killers. Close combat is probably the most intense, fearful and horrible of all life experiences. What is hard to understand for those who have not been in such situations is the fatigue of battle. When there is a pause in the fighting and the adrenaline stops pumping, an overwhelming exhaustion sets in.

Military history is replete with examples of armies that won battles and then sat down to rest. They failed to pursue the fleeing forces. Had they done so, they would have won the entire war. In a similar way, many casualties have happened when soldiers received the news that they would be going home soon. Their minds began to settle on the comforts of loved ones, family and home, rather than on the task still at hand. Carelessness caused them to miss the journey home. Forever, in some cases.

Combat is certainly not a spectator sport, as some Washington socialites learned during the battle of Bull Run at the start of the Civil War. They ventured out from the capital to watch the spectacle from a nearby hillside, the way we would turn out to watch a football game. It promised to be entertaining. But war is no game. The Union soldiers broke ranks and retreated faster than the spectators could withdraw. The Confederates won a significant victory that day but rested while Washington, D.C., lay open before them. Had they pursued their adversaries into the city, the Civil War would have been a very short war. Instead, six hundred and fifty thousand Americans died before it ended. The Northern states eventually prevailed, of course, and were able to preserve the Union.

It takes inner strength and vigilance to execute a war. For the Christian, inner peace in the midst of our conflict is possible because the Bible says, "He has overcome the world" (John 16:33).

Jesus the Warrior

In Greek culture, redemption was a military concept. When a battle was won, the victors gathered up many of the vanquished and took them off as slaves. Some of those captives would be men or women of rank and importance who usually did not make very good slaves. They were, however, of great value to those left behind in their homeland. In such cases, the victors would let it be known that they were willing to release certain captives—for a price. This process was called *redemption,* and the price that was paid was called the *ransom.* Many teachers of the early Church saw our redemption this way.

In the ransom-redemption perspective of atonement, Jesus gave Himself up as a ransom—a kind of prisoner exchange. As the Scriptures say, "For even the Son of Man did not come to be served, but to serve, and to give his life as a ransom for many" (Mark 10:45).

Satan, delighted over his victory, was tricked, and his plan backfired. Jesus defeated Satan and set the captives free from bondage.

Imagine a recently released action movie (produced by the never-existent Jackson Production Company) in which Arnold Schwarzenegger is exchanged for the release of Pee Wee Herman. The captors are excited to get their hands on Schwarzenegger as Herman wipes his sweaty brow and thanks God for deliverance. In minutes, the heavily muscled captive's docile appearance is transformed into the ultimate warrior. As Arnold defeats the criminal mastermind, we get a glimpse of the ransom-redemption view of life.

"I owed a debt I could not pay; He paid a debt that He did not owe" are the words to an old hymn.[1] These words are as true now as they ever have been. Our joy is based upon the fact that because of Jesus' victory, we are allowed to trade our sorrows for His joy. We trade our defeat for His victory. We trade our ignominy and shame for His favor! Not only did the ancients hold this view, but classic reformers of the Church did as well.

Martin Luther held the same view. He reflected these ideas in his most famous hymn "A Mighty Fortress Is Our God." The lyrics include the phrases "And He [Jesus] must win the battle" and "For lo, his [Satan's] doom is sure; one little word shall fell him."

To Luther and many early Church fathers, redemption is to be understood in terms of spiritual warfare. The whole life of Christ was also seen as a glorious act of strategic genius by those patriarchs of Christianity.

With this in mind, consider Jesus on the eve of His greatest battle. Where did He get the strength? The book of Hebrews tells us:

> Let us fix our eyes on Jesus, the author and perfecter of our faith, who for the joy set before him endured the

cross, scorning its shame, and sat down at the right hand of the throne of God.

Hebrews 12:2

Like Jesus, we are strengthened not only by our present joy but also by the joy we anticipate when our mission is accomplished. If we are not focused on the end goal and the joy that will come at the completion, our prayer in the midst of trials will be "Lord, just get me out of this!"

All warfare, whether ancient or modern, seen or unseen, shares a common factor: battle fatigue. Fighting the fight of faith can be exhilarating at first. A new Christian coming from a relatively sheltered environment may boldly rebuke the devil for causing traffic lights to turn red on his or her way to the Bible study. On the other hand, people who have struggled for decades with difficult life situations know the emotional and spiritual fatigue of unseen warfare. Seasoned veterans like these know well this key fact about spiritual warfare and spiritual warriors: Their strength is in the joy of the Lord alone.

The Warrior's Source of Strength

Trials are not necessarily spiritual warfare, in the sense that there is a demon behind every difficult situation. But in the midst of trials, large or small, there is always pressure warring against your faith, your loyalty to others and your dedication to Christ. Some trials last a very long time. Or at least it seems like a long time. Sometimes spiritual warfare is like a siege. Manifold trials assault you like wave after wave of charges against your defenses. In such situations, you had better have learned to tap into the joy of the Lord, or the attacks against faith and hope will eventually wear you down and you will be overrun.

Are you going through long-term financial pressure? Just when you seem to be getting over it, something else unexpected happens—the car breaks down, the house needs repairs, that pair of shoes wears out. It would be easier if there were not this seesaw effect. We sometimes feel as though we take two steps forward and one step back. People who struggle with their weight, as I have over the years, often experience many of the same kinds of frustration. I have probably lost three tons during the last ten years. A final victory is what everyone in these situations longs for. If we are not careful, it is at those moments that depression and pressure cause us to make some irrational decisions.

The Strength of Joy

The word *joy* is used 61 times in the New International Version of the New Testament. Joy is often contrasted with the concepts of affliction and tribulation. Spiros Zodhiates says of the Greek words for *affliction* and *tribulation:*

> To the early Christians [these words] meant not so much ill health, poverty, or loss of friends, but the sacrifices they had to make and the perils they had to meet from their proclamations of profession of Christ.[2]

John's first epistle was written for the stated purpose of strengthening the Church with joy: "These things write we unto you that your joy may be full" (1 John 1:4, KJV). The apostle Paul saw imparting the strength found in joy as part of his ministry to the early churches. He wrote to the church at Philippi: "Convinced of this, I know that I will remain, and I will continue with all of you for your progress and joy in the faith" (Philippians 1:25). And to the church at Corinth: "Not that we lord it over your faith, but we work with you for your joy, because it is by faith you stand firm" (2 Corinthians 1:24).

Paul put a premium on joy because he knew that they would need it as a source of strength for the battles ahead. When you have the joy of the Lord in the middle of affliction, it becomes contagious. If you are going through a difficult battle as a group of believers, just one person with faith, the joy of the Lord and a gift of encouragement can mean the difference between victory and defeat. Paul wrote to the church at Thessalonica concerning its joyful attitude:

> You became imitators of us and of the Lord; in spite of severe suffering, you welcomed the message with the joy given by the Holy Spirit. And so you became a model to all the believers in Macedonia and Achaia.
>
> 1 Thessalonians 1:6–7

No great battle is won without great sacrifice. Motivated by the joy set before Him, Jesus made the supreme sacrifice and won the supreme victory over Satan. After that, He ascended to the throne on high and sat down at the right hand of God. Godly goals give a sense of meaning and purpose to our lives. They also enable us to endure all types of hardship. It is important to note that Jesus was not following His own career plans; it was the Father who set the goals before Him.

God's goals for our lives are often radically different from the world's standards. By those standards, it is okay to follow Christ as long as it does not require significant sacrifice. Those who respond to God's calling and wholly dedicate their lives to Christ are considered to be "wasting their lives" by those with a mindset of this present world. Such people cannot relate to those who do not consider self-preservation and self-advancement their highest priorities. Sacrifice does not make sense to people who do not see the joy set before them. You can try to explain, but in the end, until they personally meet Jesus Christ, they will never understand.

There are six principles to achieving the inner strength that every Christian needs: (1) fight your way out of a siege; (2) find the joy of camaraderie; (3) maintain ranks in the face of battle; (4) remember the big picture; (5) use the power of consistent focus; and (6) stay connected to the source of joy. Let's explore each of these principles.

Fight Your Way Out of a Siege

If you examine Philippians 4 and Colossians 3, you will find a progression of prayer that will enable you to escape the hold of chronic problems. In some cases, such ongoing problems are a result of spiritual captivity. This kind of captivity, however, may not be due to disobedience but due to the enemy's constant barrage of depression and despair. The key Scripture passage is from Paul's letter to the Philippians:

> Do not be anxious about anything, but in everything, by prayer and petition, with thanksgiving, present your requests to God. And the peace of God, which transcends all understanding, will guard your hearts and your minds in Christ Jesus. Finally, brothers, whatever is true, whatever is noble, whatever is right, whatever is pure, whatever is lovely, whatever is admirable—if anything is excellent or praiseworthy—think about such things.
>
> Philippians 4:6–8

Another way of saying it is, "Be full of care for nothing." The Living Bible paraphrases the text this way:

"Don't worry about anything but pray about everything." This warning against chronic worry is juxtaposed with the exhortation to prayer and supplication. Instead of being consumed by the former, do the latter. Pray in everything. In everything, that is, that you have been so accustomed to fretting about. Paul exhorts his readers to use the mental assault of the enemy to signal a retreat into the presence of God. I heard someone say once that if Satan knew we would retreat to prayer every time we are tempted, he might change his tactics, for he hates it when we pray. Seeking the presence of God in difficult times turns worry and despair into peace "which transcends all understanding." In other words, a supernatural peace.

Thanksgiving should be made to the Father for His faithfulness and for the answer to prayers not yet received. This will move us further into God's presence, as well as His peace and joy.

One of the problems with the concept of faith, as it is taught by many, is that there is no clear distinction between attitude management techniques and what is purely biblical faith. Managing our attitudes is very important—even essential—to being a good soldier. "Be-positive" motivational techniques, however, are not in themselves keys to releasing the supernatural power of God.

The supernatural peace of God, which comes from His presence, is able to do far more than a peace that comes from attitude management. Paul wrote:

> I pray that out of his glorious riches he may strengthen you with power through his Spirit in your inner being . . . and to know this love that surpasses knowledge—that you may be filled to the measure of all the fullness of God.
>
> Ephesians 3:16, 19

God's peace will "keep your hearts and minds through Christ Jesus." The Greek word translated here as "keep" is the word *phroureo*. It means "to guard or protect with a military guard." In other words, do whatever you must do to keep your heart in that place of spiritual peace because it guards your inner man as if it were being guarded by a great military force.

Paul echoes this same idea in his letter to the Colossians: "Let the peace of Christ rule in your hearts, since as members of one body you were called to peace. And be thankful" (Colossians 3:15). The Greek word translated as "rule" is *brabeuo*. It means "to be an umpire" or "to decide, determine or to rule." It comes from a root word *brabeion*, which refers to a prize someone would win in a contest. Those who rule (*brabeuo*) their hearts will win the prize (*brabeion*).

Find the Joy of Camaraderie

Meaningful fellowship with the saints is an important source of God's joy. When things are going bad, when problems are all around me, my tendency is to retreat into myself. I do not want to relate to anybody; I do not want to talk to anybody; I just want to go off and be alone. I have had to remind myself that while some relationships are a drain to me, others are sources of supply.

How many times I have heard my wife tell me, "Harry, you know you're getting a little bit beside yourself. I think you need to go see Brother Gary!" Gary pastored a church about an hour and a half away from us in upstate New York. We would periodically go off to a conference together or just spend a couple of hours over lunch. Whether we discussed any particular problem bothering me or not, I always came back refreshed and full of joy. Joy in your life builds as you learn to balance your relationships between those you have the privilege of pouring your life into and those who pour theirs into yours. If you become unbalanced in either direction, you will begin to lose the joy of your salvation.

There is no greater joy than seeing those you have ministered to growing in the Lord and becoming disciples of Jesus with warriors' hearts. These amazing champions can extend God's Kingdom. In the first chapter I noted the meaning of the Greek word *huios*, which is translated "son." It implies a mature son who is also a warring son.

Paul wrote to the Thessalonian Christians whom he had birthed into the Kingdom, "For what is our hope, our joy or the crown in which we will glory in the presence of our Lord Jesus when he comes? Is it not you? Indeed, you are our glory and joy" (1 Thessalonians 2:19–20). The apostle John wrote to the elder Gaius: "I have no greater joy than to hear that my children walk in truth" (3 John 4).

Psalm 126:6 (KJV) speaks to this principle. It states very clearly that those who go forth and "plant precious seeds with weeping" shall undoubtedly come again *with rejoicing*, bringing their sheaves with them. Personal ministry, evangelism and serving others are not convenient. They take wisdom, skill and focus.

It is so easy to take a step back from sharing the Gospel and caring for others. Spectators do sense some measure of joy when their side is winning. But they will never, never know the joy of victory over the enemy until they find their places and fulfill their callings. Have you lost the joy of your salvation? The best way to stir it up is to find a way to serve those who need to receive Christ or who have just been saved.

Not everyone is called to be a pastor or an evangelist. Your contribution may be through a gift of helps, administration or encouragement. But know this for sure:

God has a place for everyone in the ongoing advancement of the Kingdom.

Maintain Ranks in the Face of Battle

In the midst of both trials and triumphs, continue to keep the commandments of God if you do not want to lose your joy. Disobedience will lead to bondage. There is a difference between being in a trial of faith and being in captivity as judgment for sin. You can still rejoice in the trial, but there is no joy in captivity. The plaintive tones of Psalm 137 graphically illustrate this. The exiled psalmist appears to have written near the end of the Jews' captivity in Babylon.

> By the rivers of Babylon we sat and wept when we remembered Zion. There on the poplars we hung our harps, for there our captors asked us for songs, our tormentors demanded songs of joy; they said, "Sing us one of the songs of Zion!" How can we sing the songs of the LORD while in a foreign land?
>
> Psalm 137:1–4

People become captives because they have disobeyed God's Word or refused the leading and convicting of the Holy Spirit. But God is merciful, just as He was to the Jews in Babylon. He will forgive us when we repent and deliver us in spite of shortcomings.

Remember the Big Picture

Focus on the glory of God in times of trials, when you are under spiritual assault. God's glory, not our agenda, is the big-picture goal. John the Baptist is a good example here. After his purpose was fulfilled, his ministry was destined to diminish. When this began to happen, John said to his disciples, "He must become greater; I must become less" (John 3:30). John described his outlook on ministry by using the illustration of a bridegroom and his friend:

> The bride belongs to the bridegroom. The friend who attends the bridegroom waits and listens for him, and is full of joy when he hears the bridegroom's voice. That joy is mine, and it is now complete.
>
> John 3:29

Your motive for service (His glory or your glory) will certainly determine how you serve. Mercenaries are soldiers who serve for hire. They have no cause or joy set before them other than their own profit; consequently, mercenaries are not willing to sacrifice, suffer or endure. Using another analogy, Jesus said:

> The hired hand is not the shepherd who owns the sheep. So when he sees the wolf coming, he abandons the sheep and runs away. Then the wolf attacks the flock and scatters it. The man runs away because he is a hired hand and cares nothing for the sheep.
>
> John 10:12–13

It is true that a lot of fame and glory can be obtained in the process of following Christ. But a disciple with a warrior's heart keeps his eyes on God's glory—not his own.

This is a real challenge for me. At times, the last thing I think about is the glory of God. I tend to think more about accomplishing objectives for the Kingdom. God will be glorified by the decisive advances I make, right? In fact, the truth may be just the opposite. He may actually lead us into tenuous places, places of pressure, to produce His glory. From our limited perspectives, that can be hard to understand, but God sees what is in each person's heart as clearly as He sees the visible advances of the Kingdom. Winning internal spiritual battles is just as significant to Him as the outward advances—perhaps even more so.

Sometimes it is hard to know your own motives. The focus of your prayer life, however, is one indicator. If your praying is driven by your own wish list, then it is probably an indication that your life is focused on self. Praying according to God-centered priorities and God-given goals refocuses your attention on the joy set before you. When those prayers are answered, you get a taste of that joy. Jesus said to the disciples, "Until now you have not asked for anything in my name. Ask and you will receive, and your joy will be complete" (John 16:24).

The joy of the Lord strengthens our hearts when God answers prayers offered in accordance with God-given goals. Oh, how we need that kind of flow in our lives! We need to be able to rejoice in the fact that God is with us in the long-term challenges of life. We need to experience the joy of abandoning ourselves to Him and His purposes, then seeing God take up the burden of providing all that we need.

Use the Power of Consistent Focus

To have an ongoing supply of joy and strength, you have to stay focused on the prize. There are times we need to stop and calculate what it will take to accomplish an objective. Jesus said:

> Suppose a king is about to go to war against another king. Will he not first sit down and consider whether he is able with ten thousand men to oppose the one coming against him with twenty thousand?
>
> Luke 14:31

There are times when God sets the goals before you, and it is no longer a question of *if,* but *how.* When God sovereignly set the Promised Land as the goal for the children of Israel, they needed to keep their focus on the promise, not the walled cities or the giants.

Led by the Holy Spirit, Paul pressed on toward Jerusalem in spite of the looming difficulties. In Miletus, where he had stopped to visit with the elders from nearby Ephesus, he said:

> And now, compelled by the Spirit, I am going to Jerusalem, not knowing what will happen to me there. I only know that in every city the Holy Spirit warns me that prison and hardships are facing me.
>
> Acts 20:22–23

Paul's singleness of focus is expressed in the following passage:

> Brothers, I do not consider myself yet to have taken hold of it. But one thing I do: Forgetting what is behind and straining toward what is ahead, I press on toward the goal to win the prize for which God has called me heavenward in Christ Jesus.
>
> Philippians 3:13–14

How different is this from many modern ideas about God's guidance! Paul was determined to experience the joy of completion. "Certainly God wouldn't lead you into a situation where you would end up in prison," many might argue. Not Paul. His heart and mind were fixed on a divinely inspired direction. He knew what lay ahead of him in Jerusalem, and I am sure many tried to dissuade him; nevertheless, Paul refused to be diverted from his course.

Paul's response to what surely lay ahead was, "None of these things move me, neither count I my life dear unto myself, so that I might finish my course with joy" (Acts 20:24, KJV). Paul was saying, in effect, that his goal was to reach his destination, even if it meant giving up his own life. Thus, he did not alter his course because of his fears or people's well-intended advice. Paul remained focused on his God-given goal just as Jesus did when Peter urged Him to save Himself from the cross.

Stay Connected to the Source of Joy

Beholding "the joy that is set before us" requires a measure of spiritual revelation because it is certainly not always going to make sense to the natural mind. That is why it is so important that we maintain a regular prayer life. Without prayer and communion with God, the vision begins to fade. When the vision and the incremental goals God has set before us get blurred, we naturally gravitate back to self-centeredness, and our goal again becomes saving our own lives. Communing with God in His manifest presence releases deep, supernatural joy. The joy we need oftentimes cannot be found in the natural realms alone, especially when we are dealing with supernatural attacks.

There have been several periods in my life when it looked as if I was being defeated on all fronts. Things were falling apart at the church, things seemed out of control at home and I was taking some hard hits financially. It was as if the enemy was overrunning my perimeter defenses on all sides. When it seems that every area of your life is under attack, it is hard to find a place to get away from it. The tendency of the flesh is to retreat to a position not under attack. If things are going badly at work, you go home. If things are not good at home, you go fishing. If the weather is too bad for fishing, you go to the movies and so on. When there are attacks everywhere at once, you might ask, "God, why are You letting this happen?" Maybe it is so that you can learn to run to Him.

What I find in these situations is how to use the wonderful power of praise and worship as a means of moving into a spiritual place where there is faith and joy. Several years ago I went through one of these seasons. After a hectic day I would sit down to eat with my family. I had been internalizing so much stress, however, that when I tried to eat my stomach would cramp up. The only way I was able to work through that period was to begin praying on my drive home.

In my particular spiritual battle, I found that scriptural meditation enabled me to draw strength and joy from the presence of God. Driving home, I would think on a Scripture that seemed to provide an answer to one of my problems. I would recite it over and over again. Then I would pray the Scripture, confess it, claim it and do battle with it against the enemy. When you are in the car by yourself, you can get really loud without worrying about what others think. In the face of despair, I would cry out things like:

"You have made known to me the path of life; you will fill me with joy in your presence, with eternal pleasures at your right hand" (Psalm 16:11).

"With joy you will draw water from the wells of salvation" (Isaiah 12:3).

"And the disciples were filled with joy and with the Holy Spirit" (Acts 13:52).

"For the kingdom of God is not a matter of eating and drinking, but of righteousness, peace and joy in the Holy Spirit" (Romans 14:17).

I learned to walk out Psalm 100 in a practical way. This psalm says three things clearly: (1) Enter His gates with thanksgiving; (2) Enter His courts with praise; and (3) Bless His name. For me, this meant I would have to choose something from my day to be thankful about. As I would meditate on that specific issue, verbalizing my thanksgiving was key. Like stepping onto the first step of an escalator, giving heartfelt thanks creates a sense of ascent into God's presence. Next I would continue deeper into the presence of God by offering praise, which in my mind means bragging on Him. A praise session might include a statement like this: "Just as You opened the Red Sea as a way of deliverance for Moses, You have given me favor with creditors and the IRS."

Finally, worship that releases joy would reach its climax as I would talk to God about His character. "Lord, You are always there. There is none like You! You are faithful and true in everything You do." This kind of communication with God is what the psalmist meant by "blessing His name." We are raving about His character the way my wife likes me to recite the reasons why I love her.

As you can tell from this description of my prayer time, laboring to enter God's rest (see Hebrews 4:11) is not primarily about struggling with the devil. It is about reconnecting with Jesus by the power of the Holy Spirit.

The forces of depression and despair had blocked my entrance into the presence of God. I had to employ the sword of the Spirit, which is the Word of God (see Ephesians 6:17), to fight my way through to the place where I could receive the strength that comes from the fullness of joy.

Victories in the Kingdom of God and victories over our personal adversary, the devil, are progressive. We win one battle and take one hill at a time. The celebrations are short and sweet. Time comes quickly to move on to the next battle. It is easy to think that if you were to conquer all the problems that you are facing right now, life would be easy. Not so. There are other adversaries out there waiting for you. When you come to the new battles, go back again to step one. Do not let the assaults worry you. Use them as signals to run to the presence of God with prayer and thanksgiving. Worship and praise are vital parts of our warfare.

4

The Character of a Christian Warrior

Brokenness, Dependence and Strength

The battle, sir, is not to the strong alone; it is to the vigilant, the active, the brave. . . .[1]

Patrick Henry

At the opening of the 2003 Iraq war, an unthinkable attack occurred. One of our own men allegedly attacked us from the inside, breaking the soldiers' sacred bond of trust. His targets were officers. Lashing out at those he had vowed to follow, he allegedly lobbed hand grenades into a command tent where officers lay sleeping. Sixteen were wounded. Two men died.

Who would have committed such an act?

And why?

To the world, it appeared that an American, seduced by enemy propaganda, changed loyalties. Past hurts and resentments perhaps played a role. In the final analysis, only God really knows. Whatever the reason, there is an important lesson to be learned for Christian soldiers. Because, you see, we are just as vulnerable to being taken captive emotionally and psychologically as that soldier seems to have been.

Indeed. In the spiritual war that every believer is involved in, there will be moments when our allies mysteriously turn against us. During counseling sessions, many wives tell me that they never suspected that their husbands would cheat, divorce or abandon them and their kids. Other believers have experienced betrayal on the job. You put trust in a fellow worker and suddenly he or she ambitiously leaps for opportunities at your expense.

No level of Christian service seems exempt from these mysterious attacks. Deacons, elders or even pastors can seemingly change overnight. Although we are wearing the Christian "uniform" of church attendance, service or other forms of religious activity, our inner lives may be tormented by mood swings and meditation on enemy propaganda.

The remainder of this chapter will emphasize the character traits that will keep you from becoming a prisoner of war in your heart and mind. Let me remind you that the purpose of this book is to think through one of the many aspects of our relationship with God—what it means for disciples to be as soldiers and the Church to be as an army. It is important to note up front that people can get into trouble when they begin to "do theology by analogy." That happens when a parable or a metaphor is used as a means to crank out theological interpretations that go far beyond the intended meaning. Because the Christian as a warrior is one of many metaphors used to explain what it means to be a disciple, "warrior-hood" needs to be kept in balance with other aspects of God's truth.

There are so many facets to the purpose and person of God that no one analogy or metaphor can begin to paint the entire picture. Jesus, for example, is called both the Lamb of God and the Lion of Judah, the Captain of the Heavenly Hosts and the Good Shepherd, the Messianic King and the Suffering Servant. He is Bridegroom to the Church and the Brother of us all. As followers of Christ, we are referred to as students, athletes, farmers, soldiers and sheep.

The apostle Paul shares a powerful insight in 1 Corinthians 13. If we do not have love as the foundation of our walks with God, he notes, we can pollute even the most powerful gifts. Prophecy can become a mistrusted manifestation because of the pollution of a life devoid of love. Miracles are frequently discounted because of carnival-like figures who masquerade as servants of God—selling their powers for bags of gold. To avoid these blatant misrepresentations of the nature of God, our warfare concepts must be balanced.

With this balance in mind, remember that the Church is called to be both a family and an army. When people focus on only one dimension of Christian life, they lose perspective on how to function properly in the body. Generals are very good at giving orders, but the Christian leader, who is a general, is also a part of the Church. He is also a father in a family. If he does not know how to be a father, general, CEO and friend at the same time, his ministry will suffer. Real-life generals who do not know how to change roles when they get home, usually make poor fathers and destroy their families.

Understanding that there are many ways to define our identities as Christians, let's look a bit more closely at what God has to say about being soldiers of the cross. The best way to do this is to zero in on the natural soldier. What is he like? What makes him tick? Answering these questions will lead us in the right direction.

The Christian as Spiritual Warrior

Steven Spielberg's *Saving Private Ryan* portrayed the invasion of Normandy in a way that most people had never seen before. As graphic as the footage was of the landing on Omaha Beach, what actually happened was many times worse. In the movie, about 75 actors were "shot or wounded" landing on Omaha; about two hundred others were seen lying on the ground. Breaking through the enemy defenses to get off the beach took 26 minutes. In 1944, it took seven hours, in which time more than seven thousand were killed and thousands more wounded. Was victory that day worth the enormous price?

In light of history, the answer is a very painful yes. No one in his right mind goes to war for fun, excitement or glory. There is great sacrifice, which must be measured by the value of the mission. What is at stake in our warfare is the eternal destiny of millions. Similarly, there have been many casualties in our war against the powers of darkness.

Today's churches are filled with people carrying deep emotional and spiritual wounds because of this war. Marriages have been shattered, best friends have separated and businesses have collapsed. These are significant battles on a personal basis. Further, many formerly devout people have died on the battlefield. These folks no longer attend church, they sneer at preachers and almost deny the existence of God. The realities of natural war should sound an alarm to the Body of Christ.

Although warfare is intensely negative, spiritual warfare can have value. Our big-picture goal is for people empowered by the Holy Spirit to acquire greater influence. If genuine Christians are strategically placed as governmental leaders, educators and corporate leaders, our society can be transformed.

For the grand scheme to be carried out, we have to know what to do at the ground level. Transforming society is a big goal. This transformation will occur one day at a time, one person at a time, one relationship at a time, one job at a time. What we need are sold-out individuals making the Gospel tangible.

The Lord has a significant problem in the world today. How can God have a problem? His children are reluctant to see their lives from His perspective. Despite our prayers and faith affirmations, it takes God-given vision to view the unique importance of our current stations in life. Even if you are on an express train to fame and glory, Christian greatness lies in your attention to mundane details. Most of us do not expect to be used significantly by God because we have an improper vision of our function as spiritual warriors.

Characteristics of a Warrior

The terms *warfare* and *warriors* imply confrontation. Indeed, Jesus Himself said, "The kingdom of heaven has been forcefully advancing, and forceful men lay hold of it" (Matthew 11:12). It would, however, be a big mistake to adopt an aggressive style, a sort of "Sherman-tank-in-the-china-shop" approach. Adopt that kind of attitude and you will find yourself becoming less like Christ and more like a warrior in some barbarian horde. Like Attila the Hun, you will take no prisoners, kill your wounded and slaughter a lot of innocent people along the way.

The warrior heart is characterized not by a violent, aggressive personality, but first and foremost by self-mastery. In that sense, it is a perfect paradigm for Christian discipleship. One fruit of the Holy Spirit is meekness. Not to be confused with weakness, meekness is defined as "power under control."

To be the kind of people that the Holy Spirit can lead into spiritual warfare, we must develop the heart, the attitude and the self-mastery of a warrior. Galatians 4:6 says, "Because you are sons, God sent the Spirit of his Son into our hearts, the Spirit who calls out, 'Abba, Father.'" A careful study of the Greek word *huios*, which is translated here as "son," implies a mature son. A mature son can receive the blessing of an inheritance. He must also shoulder the responsibility of defending that inheritance. If necessary, he is also a warring son.

When we come to full maturity, we are not only able to be hearers of the Word, but we are able to live it out, to "war" with it. In a parallel sense, soldiers and Christians are entrusted with power, authority and weapons of warfare in proportion to their self-mastery. Understanding this is key. Soldiers who achieve their maximum potential have passed through certain qualifying stages of both maturity and skill.

Gordon Dalby in his book *Healing the Masculine Soul* examined the Green Beret as an example of today's ultimate warrior and cited six characteristics that parallel the traits of a disciple of Jesus Christ.[2] They are listed in the sections below.

Loyalty

One characteristic of the armies of the West is that its soldiers do not leave comrades behind. It is a fundamental mandate of every unit. That ideal becomes a rule for Christian warriors as well.

There are many ways to describe loyalty. The Bible gives us a paradigm for this character attribute. It is called "covenant." There is a sense that we can be in covenant with both God and man. Our biblically based covenant with God has two essential commandments: (1) love God and (2) love man (see Matthew 27:37–39). Many people describe a family-like commitment to fellow Christians as "being in covenant."

King David built his entire military strength around this concept of covenant and the willingness to lay down one's life for one's friends. On one occasion he simply remarked that he would love to have a drink of water from a certain well in his native town of Bethlehem. Three of his mighty men decided to make his wish reality. They risked life and limb in such a reckless manner that David could not in good conscience drink the water. He poured it out on the ground to symbolize that no one except God was worth the kind of risks these men took (see 2 Samuel 23:14–17). These soldiers had become loyal to a fault. Similarly, a handful of people will go overboard with covenant commitments and blame others for their excesses.

Patience or Steadfastness

Timing is everything—in warfare, in business and in Christian growth. One of the most important parts of a battle plan is coordinating the sequence of events. All things do not happen at once. If a field commander or even a single soldier gets too impatient to wait for the right timing, he can endanger thousands of lives. A Christian who is unwilling to persevere through the training and wait for the right timing may find himself facing an enemy he is unprepared to resist.

You have probably heard stories of Japanese soldiers stationed on remote islands, defending their positions many years after the war was over. A good soldier knows what it means to pursue an objective until it is taken and to hold it until relieved. His orders do not have to be reissued every day to keep him on the mission. One of the biggest tests we will face as Christians is to keep on doing what God has called us to do, even though it may seem as though we have been abandoned.

Intensity

The most difficult soldier to defeat is one who is fighting on his own soil. There is no ambiguity in his mind about what he is fighting for. To the soldiers of the invading force, the personal cause and purpose for their mission may not be so clear.

A Green Beret or a good disciple of Jesus Christ is passionate about who he is and what he does. In that context, he is willing to make great sacrifices. There are some things I would die for in God. What about you?

Calmness and Peace

Jesus told His disciples in Matthew 10 to go and preach to the lost sheep of the house of Israel. Houses that received them would get an unexpected blessing: The peace of those disciples was supposed to settle in the homes of their new converts. Christians are called to bring God's peace and order into atmospheres filled with chaos. Possessing intensity and zeal, calmness and peace, all at the same time, can be tricky.

As we think about the Church as an army, we should remember that everyone is wired differently. Not everyone will be inclined to run to the battle as quickly as you; not everyone is as quick to turn to Jesus as you were. Sometimes zeal comes as an intercessory burden; consequently, you have to know when to unload your intensity in the prayer closet and trust God to move in the hearts of others. Some Christian warriors get so consumed with their mission (myself included) that they easily lose patience with those who are not responding enthusiastically. They are so "on fire" for Jesus that they burn out. You have to realize that God is in this battle with you. Peace and calmness are the characteristics of a Christian warrior who puts his whole trust in his Commander in Chief.

Compassion

Soldiers are motivated by zeal for the cause and the mission, but they should be controlled and restrained by compassion. How many times have you heard stories of armies who, after having defeated an enemy, raped the women, massacred any survivors and burned the cities? Only good soldiers can walk in power and compassion.

Jamilah Kathem from Iraq knows about this more than most people. On April 2, 2003, the Fifteenth MEU surgeons helped to deliver her six-pound baby girl, named Rogenia. Imagine the picture: A Marine soldier happened upon a young woman in labor, desperately struggling to avoid losing her first child. The soldier could have ignored this need or, even worse, he could have lashed out in fear and hurt this defenseless mom. Days before, several of his commanders had been blown up as they attempted to help a struggling man in a car. Compassion moved these Marines to make sure that Rogenia entered the world safely.

Anyone can have zeal, especially when his life is being threatened, but good disciples, like well-trained soldiers, are ruled and controlled by love. Paul wrote that you can do many great heroic things, but if you do not have love, you will just make a lot of noise (see 1 Corinthians 13). Christian warriors who do not possess great compassion appear to the world as angry, religious zealots.

The Strength of Will

"Endure hardship with us like a good soldier of Christ Jesus" (2 Timothy 2:3). Soldiers and disciples will both go through hardships. The good ones, however, are characterized by an immovable resolve, and they never give up. There are times when it is smart to retreat to a more defensible position to rethink your strategy and tactics. There are also times when you just need to hang in there, no matter what. That kind of determination was expressed by Winston Churchill in a speech to the House of Commons on June 4, 1940:

> We shall not flag or fail. We shall go to the end. We shall fight in France, we shall fight on the seas and oceans, we shall fight with growing confidence and growing strength in the air, we shall defend our island whatever the cost may be. We shall fight on the beaches, we shall fight on the landing grounds, we shall fight in the streets, we shall fight in the hills. We shall never, never surrender.[3]

Boot Camp and Discipleship

In boot camp, all the recruitment rhetoric gives way to a sudden and rude awakening of the realities of the military. The drill sergeant's objective is to reshape recruits' thinking completely and to make them soldiers who are loyal, responsible, selflessly dedicated and equipped for any situation. That is not unlike the call to discipleship. In both cases, there is a brokenness that prepares us for warfare and service. It is the first step of self-mastery. Without this kind of inner boot camp experience, a Christian will have a mixed spirit. All of us have seen people with an outward expression of selfless service, but what comes across is mixed with self-serving motivation. When you come in contact with people who have a mixed spirit, it is often hard to put your finger on what it is that you sense, but you know intuitively that something is wrong.

There have been times in my life when I have moved in the fruit of brokenness and times when I know that I was being driven by self. It is not always easy to identify how, but I can feel the spiritual conflict. My emotions give me signs of trouble just as my physical body sends pain signals when I am injured. These are times when the self-examination process is most important.

Whenever the Holy Spirit reveals the sources of un-brokenness, it needs to be followed by deep repentance, not only for what we have done but for the general reliance and focus upon self. God wants to deal with the un-brokenness in our lives because these areas are stumbling blocks. I am sure recruits would find boot camp to be a much more pleasant experience if the drill sergeants would show a little more sympathy and understanding about their needs. But the drill sergeant's job is to train soldiers, and if he does not deal with the un-brokenness, it could cost them their lives. The Scriptures say, "My son, do not make light of the Lord's discipline, and do not lose heart when he rebukes you, because the Lord disciplines those he loves, and he punishes everyone he accepts as a son" (Hebrews 12:5–6).

To deal with the lack of self-mastery or mixed spirit, first of all, you need to examine your life for things you condemn in others. This is something I have to do regularly. It is much more important that we consecrate our own lives before God. To remove the mote from my own eye (see Matthew 7:1–5), there may have to be a painful process of self-examination. In 1 Corinthians 11:31–32, Paul says that we are to judge ourselves so that we will not be judged.

Second, let your life come under the discipline of the Holy Spirit. Spend time with God, not just talking about what you want, but listening for both His correction and direction.

Third, make it your habit to obey completely and immediately before the word is stolen from your heart.

The results of this boot-camp experience with the Holy Spirit are that (1) we communicate Christ to others with a pure, unmixed spirit; (2) we have a closer and freer relationship with the Lord; (3) we have a greater sensitivity to the inner voice; and (4) we have a greater capacity to experience the deep, inward joy of the Holy Spirit.

Don't Become a Prisoner of War

Deep repentance deals with iniquity or the twistedness of our character. That same twistedness, if not brought under the rule of Christ, can become the enemy's playground. The easiest way to become a tool of the enemy is to yield to habitual sins. The penalty for physical sins of habit are the most obvious—habitual drinkers become alcoholics, gamblers often lose their money and those indulging in pornography eventually find it affects their marriages and sex lives. Spiritual sins are often less visible than physical ones. Ironically, these spiritual sins may do the most harm.

Another way the devil takes Christians captive is by luring them into unbalanced doctrines and spiritual practices that mask, rationalize or excuse their sins. Paul wrote to Timothy:

> Those who oppose him he must gently instruct, in the hope that God will grant them repentance leading them to a knowledge of the truth, and that they will come to their senses and escape from the trap of the devil, who has taken them captive to do his will.
>
> 2 Timothy 2:25

Satan will also concentrate on the weakest point in our defense, areas where he has been able to exercise modest control. What we need to understand is that unbroken areas in our lives can become strongholds of our adversary. Once he is entrenched in that stronghold, the adversary will try to use that weakness to destroy all the blessing of God in our lives. How many times have good Christians harbored a sin of lust, anger or greed until it became a stronghold? As a result, they lost their families, their careers, their reputations or even their relationships with God. They were captives of the enemy in that they could no longer control those areas. Progressively their lives became consumed with these appetites gone wild. Habits that originally were exciting expressions of personal freedom suddenly became demanding addictions.

Let me give you a practical example of how this works. Early in my ministry there was a wave of accusations against many televangelists in the Body of Christ. The exposure of the extravagant lifestyle of one of them nearly made me stumble into a fearful mindset about pursuing media outreach. I had enjoyed his ministry from a distance for years. His failure seemed somehow personal to me. I began silently to question the motives of many of the nation's most prominent ministries. I was not alone. Nationally, many ministries recorded a marked drop in contributions and support. Even ministries with no hint of improprieties were affected. This man's personal problems were used as a weapon against the Body of Christ. Stereotyped portrayals of hypocritical ministers made their way into talk shows, comedy routines and movies.

A couple of years ago I spent some time with this same fellow at a small ministers' retreat. I was impressed with his current brokenness and contrition. He has learned his lessons and wants to extend the Kingdom of God.

Yet he cannot totally undo the damage of the scandals. Like Samson, who was blinded by his enemies, he was able to avenge the loss of his eyes, but he could not get them back.

Zephaniah 3:9 says, "Then will I purify the lips of the peoples, that all of them may call on the name of the LORD and serve him shoulder to shoulder." This is our goal. Let's listen to the voice of the Spirit and the Word. Let's purify our hearts.

Part 2

The Warrior's Relationships

5

Marching with Mutual Trust

Who Chose This Army?

What we have learned and relearned in our Army is that unit cohesion and teamwork are what give individual soldiers the confidence to use initiative, to be resourceful and to be all they can be.[1]

SMA Glen E. Morrell

On the fiftieth anniversary of D-Day, news commentator Peter Jennings interviewed a group of veterans from a Ranger battalion who had scaled the cliffs of Pointe Du Hoc on June 6, 1944. Under heavy machine-gun fire from above, they secured the strategic plateau overlooking the beaches of Normandy. The remaining survivors who were gathered there fifty years later talked about the bond they had felt with one another through all the years. Their heroism was vital to victory that day. Their shared experience forged men from different backgrounds into a fighting unit that ultimately became more of a fraternity of brothers.

Similarly, historian Stephen Ambrose has written many powerful accounts of World War II, capturing the individual acts of heroism and self-sacrifice that allowed the Allies to win. In *The Victors, Eisenhower and His Boys: The Men of World War II*, my favorite work of his, he says, "At the core, the American citizen-soldiers knew the difference between right and wrong, and they didn't want to live in a world in which wrong prevailed. So they fought, and won, and we all of us, living and yet to be born, must be forever profoundly grateful."[2]

A few pages later, he describes a touching conversation between a veteran and his grandson that catches the spirit of these men. "Grandpa, were you a hero in the war?" the boy asked. "No," he answered, "but I served in a company of heroes."[3]

It's powerful to see how Ambrose attributes the success of the Allies to both a philosophy of life and having a just cause. In a similar way, Christ calls us to amazingly important roles in history.

The Principle of Trust

In chapter 2 we discussed the reasoning behind a strict military honor code. If we as individuals are going to be dependable and trustworthy as soldiers of Christ, a personal honor code is necessary. Yet it cannot stop with the individual. The tricky part of life revolves around connecting and effectively working with others.

Soldiers must have an unquestioning trust in one another. But not all of us, in fact few of us, come into the Kingdom of God with impeccable character and credentials. Writing to one of the early Christian churches,

Paul went through a long list of various types of sinners and concluded:

> And that is what some of you were. But you were washed, you were sanctified, you were justified in the name of the Lord Jesus Christ and by the Spirit of our God.
>
> 1 Corinthians 6:11

The obvious question is, How do we capitalize on our strength of numbers and diversity of gifts? We must be sovereignly assembled if we are to have an impact. It is easy to salute the concept that we need each other, without analyzing the depth of our need.

In the spring of 1985, a significant transition occurred in my life. A nationally known Bible teacher, Judson Cornwall, came to our church for the first time. At one point, while we were chatting in private, he drew a small piece of paper from his pocket. The neatly creased sheet held ten pointers that would "help me in ministry." I was devastated by the number and the nature of his observations. I listened in shock as this man declared, "I took your request for help very seriously." I decided to swallow my pride and hear the man out. I did not waste his time or my energy on explanations or excuses.

Dr. Cornwall appeared at the car the next day with a similar list in his pocket. Although I responded as graciously as I could, I was astonished at the fact that my guest emerged with another lengthy list on the third day. I decided to receive the input that was given and see if it worked.

I knew that God had used this man in our public services. His messages had literally opened my understanding to a new dimension of personal communion with Christ. Every day between the morning and evening services, my wife and I would enter into glorious times of prayer and worship. This man's life and message affected us more than anyone else's since our salvation. To me, it was a no-brainer. I reached out and began to seek his advice and counsel. He became my mentor and eventually a spiritual father.

There are many other relationships that started out well but somehow got sidetracked. In the early days of faith, I believed in anyone who seemed to have sincere faith. Being a Christian, in my view, automatically raised the moral and ethical bar. I felt I could count on Christians more than unbelievers.

After being lied to and cheated a few times, along with several unfortunate business deals with Christians, I woke up to the fact that blanket trust was not a wise policy. Liking people and trusting them should be two very different things. Becoming more skeptical with experience, I eventually understood that there are steps that have to be taken to establish trust. I have written this chapter because many of us have been severely wounded as we connected with people. Our understanding of how trust is developed is not well defined; therefore, we make huge mistakes.

In this third millennium, the Body of Christ must achieve new territory in terms of influence. To move into that place, we will need to work as mini-teams much like the special operations people of World War II, the Iraq War and other conflicts.

Different Relationships at the Same Time

Not all of our relationships will be initiated in the same way. Those whom the Lord chooses to be part of your spiritual army unit may surprise you. Further, your relationships will take different paths. Some will deepen for certain purposes in our lives. Ignoring these key, God-ordained relationships can leave you without comrades or important reinforcements during times of trouble. Although David's family life was often a shambles, he demonstrated great wisdom in discerning God's dream team for his role as general and king.

Time and time again, David's men risked their lives for great goals. Their courage and loyalty were staggering. The Scriptures tell the story of David's three greatest warriors, Josheb-Basshebeth, Eleazar and Shammah (see 2 Samuel 23:8–11). These heroes were not born champions. They were chosen, cultivated and then commissioned to do tremendous works.

David's Example

The following story gives insight into the faith and philosophy underlying David's success with raising up champions.

> Some Gadites defected to David at his stronghold in the desert. They were brave warriors, ready for battle and able to handle the shield and spear. Their faces were the faces of lions, and they were as swift as gazelles in the mountains. . . . These Gadites were army commanders; the least was a match for a hundred, and the greatest for a thousand. . . . David went out to meet them and said to them, "If you have come to me in peace, to help me, I am ready to have you unite with me. But if you have come to betray me to my enemies when my hands are free from violence, may the God of our fathers see it and judge you."
>
> 1 Chronicles 12:8, 14, 17

The men who came to join David were impressive. They were capable of catapulting him to the next level. It was obvious to David that his time had come. He was finally going to enter into the fruit of Samuel's prophecy that he would one day be king (see 1 Samuel 16:13). But to become king in the tiny nation of Israel meant that he must lead an army. Israel has always lived on the edge, surrounded by enemies; therefore, David was assembling an army. His small band alone could never lead the entire nation. He had to make new alliances and let key people into his inner circle.

Ironically, the name Gad means "good fortune." This major tribe that came to David symbolized God's help in human form. David did not have the emotional luxury of keeping the fellowship of leaders in his troop small and cozy. Neither could he draw back in fear to avoid being wounded by someone like King Saul.

David had to exercise relational amnesia and follow the advice of Paul, who said, "I press on toward the goal to win the prize for which God has called me heavenward in Christ Jesus" (Philippians 3:14).

Allow God to Join Others to You

In seasons of rapid growth and acceleration, God can bring important people into our lives. People who perceive and support our calling. This dynamic is similar whether we are managers or ministers. The problem with being a rising star is that we cannot always see the motives driving the people who volunteer to help us.

When the Gadites came to David, they offered to fill in the blanks and take crucial spots in his army. He took a huge risk. Betrayal could have cost him his life. Even so, he put his faith in God and put the Gadites in positions of leadership. Notice what David declared would happen if the Gadites were coming to do him wrong. Because he had a pure heart, David said the Lord would "rebuke" them and their scheme. This was not simply a warning or even a veiled threat. It was a faith declaration. "God Himself will protect me" was what he declared before both God and man.

David was not living in a super-spiritual world. He wanted there to be a strong bond between the Gadites and himself. This would take time:

> If you have come to me in peace, to help me, I am ready to have you unite with me. But if you have come to betray me to my enemies when my hands are free from violence, may the God of our fathers see it and judge you.
>
> 1 Chronicles 12:17

David's plan from the beginning was that those who were to be joined together militarily would also be joined together personally. He stated from the beginning his intention of developing a spiritual covenant with all those whom God joined to him.

Our strategic Kingdom relationships are very similar to our relationships with Christ. We start out self-centered, yet under the Spirit's influence we become God-centered. Most people come to Christ for selfish motives, that is, for forgiveness, for salvation or for God's help in some area of their lives. Only afterward does the love and grace of God win their hearts. In the same way, many people become members of a church because of some need they have in their lives. Others come because they feel the call of God to that place. In either case, the knitting process David talks about is not automatic. It is something that unfolds over time.

Hearts are knit together because we make a commitment, just as in a marriage. There is often a spiritual sense of brotherhood at the outset. And I am not just talking about emotionalism. This feeling of covenant love needs to be there as both a signpost of God's dealings and the glue that connects us. We determine to work together through our difficulties. Good marriages are a blessing because husbands and wives have been working on them for years and are still in the process. This is covenant relationship.

David was able to say to Jonathan, "Thy love to me was wonderful, passing the love of women" (1 Samuel 18:1, KJV). Our basic understanding of human relationships has been so perverted by Satan that most of us cannot read this passage without thinking about a homosexual relationship. How we have been influenced by this present evil generation! I believe David and Jonathan had a deep, supportive friendship. It was a covenant relationship in which two people were bonded together for a just cause. They felt their gift of friendship to one another was among their most valuable possessions.

God will bring into your life those who will love you and whom you will love with a deep, abiding love. You will be there for each other in all kinds of situations. Ephesians 4:16 says it this way, "From him the whole body, joined and held together by every supporting ligament, grows and builds itself up in love, as each part does its work."

Building Blocks of Trust

Instant trust is impossible. Trust is typically built by a proven demonstration of skill or character. I can *love* you without trusting you, just as the spouse of a drug user loves his or her mate. And I can also *trust* you without loving you. This is why I go to well-trained doctors and blindly follow their advice, even though I do not know them. Developing a trust relationship based on character requires a different kind of focus. Truly discerning someone's character can take an enormous amount of time. Gifts, skills and ability can be proven relatively quickly.

Building or rebuilding trust is one of the most difficult tasks facing new millennium Christians. In an era where people demand instant everything, instant trust is still impossible; consequently, many people bear wounds of betrayal and disillusionment about relationships. Some vow they will never allow anyone to get close enough to hurt them again. Trust is not something that occurs automatically because people go to the same building to worship. It takes an intentional and consistent effort.

Listed below are some practical suggestions on developing trust relationships.

1. Identify God's connections. When I met Dr. Cornwall, I could have said to myself that I did not like people of his color. Or I could have recoiled at "the help" he was attempting to give. Instead I chose to make changes in my life, to receive him and to accept his input. I took a chance with my eyes wide open. Let me encourage you to do the same.

2. Be trustworthy yourself. Personal integrity is a lifestyle. Issues of honesty and faithfulness should be non-negotiable. As integrity becomes less defined and more "flexible" in a community, relationships will naturally deteriorate. The psalmist wrote, "[The Lord] despises a vile man but honors those who fear the LORD, who keeps his oath even when it hurts" (Psalm 15:4).

3. Be sincere and straightforward. Never mislead others with your words. I think it is crucial that we become committed to really speaking the truth. I am not suggesting that we speak unkindly, but flattery is actually a sinful form of deception.

4. Observe a person's unique gifts and strengths. What can this person bring to the table? If I am going to trust a person, what is it that I am going to trust? Am I going to trust his spiritual gifts? Am I going to trust her natural talents? Am I going to trust his ability in certain areas? Or am I going to trust only his or her character? Only time and experience will make that clear. We live in a generation of hype. Many boast of achievements far beyond their competence. Despite all this, there is something uniquely blessed in the lives of those around us.

5. *Give others another chance.* People make mistakes. Do not let memories of past mishaps spoil your opinion of the relationship at hand. Problems occur when hurts and unresolved issues in people's hearts cause them to jump to negative conclusions. They look for any mistake to justify the worst expectations of people. Do not let the problems in your past spoil relationships with people in the present.

Conclusion

"Let's take it to another level." This popular phrase has almost become a generational mantra. We live in a world in which simply getting more is seen as success. Yet with this highly individualistic and competitive press to go to the next level, it is interesting to note that we often need someone else's help to get there.

David was aware of his need of partners (covenant brothers), as we have seen. Our era, by contrast, is marked by broken relationships more than anything else. From divorces at home to layoffs at work, no relationship seems totally secure. Yet God has ordained connections with purpose and commitment. As I look back on more than 25 years of ministry, I am thankful that I pressed through my fears and really trusted a few strategic people.

Do not be afraid to trust again! Do not give up on your comrades in arms. The door to your destiny may be marked *Partnership, Teamwork* or *Friend.*

6

The Inner War

Mirror Image

Every man has three characters—that which he exhibits, that which he has, and that which he thinks he has.[1]

Alphonse Karr

One of the many reasons for the 9/11 tragedy was the lack of respect that the U.S. had for her opponents. We underestimated the level of hatred that Middle Eastern extremists have for America. Who would have thought that men could work for years to set up one defiant act? A handful of men killed thousands of our friends and loved ones. There was hardly a sector of society that was not touched. The reason this atrocity could be perpetrated upon New York, Washington and a field in Pennsylvania was attributed to insufficient security in U.S. airports. Our security was lax because we had no respect for the ingenuity of these men.

Today we have a healthy respect for terrorists. Many pilots now fly armed to ward off future calamities. As believers, we should attempt to protect our God-ordained relationships as vigilantly as the U.S. now protects its airports. It is a matter of respect. If we need to respect our enemies, how much more do our friends deserve our respect? In the book *In-laws, Outlaws and the Functional Family*, I shared an acrostic for relationships that will help people analyze their difficulties. The acrostic spells the word *TRUE*. It stands for Trust, Respect, Understanding and Expressed Love.

Most of our relational problems fall into one of these four categories. If I want to build or strengthen a relationship, it is necessary for me to take a moment to decide which area I should approach.

In the last chapter, we talked about the challenge of building trust with people we are called to work and fellowship with. Even a God-ordained relationship can be disrupted if we do not work at building on our early sense of connection or ongoing respect for fellow workers and friends.

Giving Respect

Everyone wants to be respected. All of us know what it feels like to be taken for granted or, even worse, abused. Trying to free yourself from a relationship that has become abusive can be risky at best.

The best way to establish a relationship with healthy boundaries is to begin the right way. Two secular entertainers epitomize two different approaches to respect and relationships. Aretha Franklin became internationally famous as she belted out her demands for respect. I would not recommend you imitate her style, but the content of her message is exemplary. Although this preacher's daughter was a little earthy in her declaration to her lover, she shows us how to begin a relationship properly.

Ms. Franklin took three insightful steps in her famous song. First, she defined what respect meant to her. In fact, she literally spelled out the word. Second, she told her man how she felt about the direction the relationship was taking. Understanding her feelings would give most men a way of identifying with her needs. In essence, she gave him a compelling reason to change. Third, she told the man in her life exactly how he could fix the problem.

Most of us lack this kind of clarity in our relationships. We meander in and out of different emotional zones. We are more like the comedian Rodney Dangerfield. Most middle-aged Americans remember this portly entertainer as someone who lamented the lack of respect that he received. Like the chorus to a song, he would frequently refrain, "I don't get no respect!"

Similar to many of us, Rodney passively received disrespect, analyzed it and then complained. Audiences all over the world have identified with his predicaments and laughed at his mournful sagas. Although the laughter of thousands is affirming, his real problems were never dealt with. The basis of comedy is often the irony of exaggerated truth. I hope for Rodney Dangerfield's sake that his stage problems were totally based in fiction.

Unfortunately, in real life there is a tendency for people to take important relationships for granted. Even the most sensitive people occasionally overlook the needs of those around them. Only Jesus would not break a bruised reed (see Matthew 12:19). He was the perfect balance of strength and gentleness. We often suffer in silence or tell our tale of woe to a handful of loyal confidants. If we are not vigilant like Aretha Franklin, we will wind up complaining like Dangerfield for the rest of our lives.

Proverbs points out the dynamics behind the respect or disrespect many of us receive:

> Wealth brings many friends, but a poor man's friend deserts him. . . . Many curry favor with a ruler, and everyone is the friend of a man who gives gifts. A poor man is shunned by all his relatives—much more do his friends avoid him! Though he pursues them with pleading, they are nowhere to be found.
>
> Proverbs 19:4, 6–7

Everybody wants to be around those who are rich, but the poor are rejected. Everything in life does not revolve around economics, but a powerful principle is revealed here. There are going to be people we deal with who seem to us to be, relatively speaking, poor. We are smarter, more gifted and more "upwardly mobile." Carnally minded people despise being with those "lower" than themselves. Such an attitude is perhaps a function of a kind of poverty in their own lives, of a poor sense of their own self-worth. They are not secure enough in themselves to associate with the poor. Jesus was, in a sense, the richest of all. Yet He came to announce Good News to the poor (see Luke 4:18). Remember, poverty is relative; someone always has more; someone always has less. God says, "He who mocks the poor shows contempt for their Maker; whoever gloats over disaster will not go unpunished" (Proverbs 17:5).

When people have a condescending attitude toward the poor, it is a telltale sign that they have forgotten how poor they are in relationship to God. They have forgotten how much they are in need of His mercy.

On occasion I have had the privilege of being in the company of some powerful and prominent individuals. If you watch closely, it is not too hard to tell who is trying to buy friendship rather than simply being friends. A lot of people are eager to gain a vicarious sense of importance through association. They fawn over people who seem to be favored, important or rich in prestige. Like teenage boys trying to get close to the prettiest girl in the class, they compete for access to these important people.

Christians, even pastors—especially pastors—are not immune to that sort of thing. In this regard we often act like the world. Many people came to Jesus, not because they loved Him in their hearts, but because He multiplied loaves and fishes. They had a selfish agenda for coming to Christ. In the same way, many want to be a friend of someone who will improve their social status.

There is nothing wrong with pursuing relationships with gifted or prominent people. If we are willing to be a blessing to these folks, God may allow us the privilege of being a confidant and friend to many. Proverbs 22:11 tells us, "He who loves a pure heart and whose speech is gracious will have the king for his friend." We must invest in our friendships with a pure heart. Violating relational protocol, however, will leave us relationally bankrupt. The sticking point is that we must learn God's protocol in relationships based on respect. True respect cannot be demanded, mandated or cajoled out of someone. Respect is earned in the hard work of relational commerce. We exchange time and energy with the right attitude for powerful, living relationships. In other words, we must give respect, if we hope to receive it.

Gaining Respect

If you are not rich and famous, you may think, "How do I *make* someone respect me? What can I do to restore respect in the relationships that really matter to me?" These are core questions that every person grapples with. Ironically, receiving respect starts on the inside—with our own attitudes.

Those who have never had the foundations of acceptance, value and purpose built in their lives are on a never-ending quest to fill the void. Lacking this foundation makes them rejection-prone. It is like a self-fulfilling prophecy. They are convinced that others do not accept them, regardless of what their friends do or say. Thus, they demand from others constant affirmation. In that sense, they are always making emotional withdrawals from their relationships and are rarely making meaningful deposits. Eventually they get so overdrawn in their relationships that their friends close the account. Then they may say, "I knew it all along; they really didn't like me." This kind of thinking makes things even worse because it justifies their negative expectations. It is sad that relationships have to end like this.

Let me give you an example of how this works. A music minister at a particular church somehow felt devalued and disrespected. Everything had begun so well. He had felt safe and shielded from the politics that typically ensnare a church music position during his three years at the church.

Later, even when he ministered his best, the senior pastor seemed to simply shrug and move on, without ever a compliment or an encouraging word. Disheartened by neglect, he began to share his negative feelings in strictest confidence with his friends in other churches. He knew that his growing negativism would eventually create problems in the church. The tensions were becoming obvious.

He typed his letter of resignation, even though he really did not have any solid leads. He simply could not stand it anymore. When the big day came for him to turn in his resignation, he received a call from a pastor at another church, wanting to interview him for a music minister's position with a great salary and benefits. This position seemed to be God's answer to a troubled situation. What deliverance!

He accepted the new position, and the first three months were glorious. His creative juices flowed again. What a delight! At the end of the first six months, though, the downward spiral began anew. Tensions began to mount. Two years later, the music minister was once again crying out to God for deliverance from a church he once loved.

In this little parable, it is easy to see how relationships can deteriorate. I am sure that both pastors misunderstood the music minister's needs. After becoming frustrated with this "temperamental" musician, the pastors let the sparks fly. The real problem, though, was an issue of respect. The music minister's feelings were often hurt, but he did not speak to the leadership team in a biblical fashion. Matthew 18 is clear. We should talk to our brother or sister one-on-one first. If this does not work, we should approach the person in the company of one trusted intermediary. The music minister could not control the stereotypes that most pastors have about musicians. But he could have chosen to work harder at communication and productivity.

Sadly, the music minister was his own worst enemy. When things got tough, he withdrew in depression. God had faithfully connected him with several major opportunities, yet he had been unable to truly settle down and build. At root, the music minister had some character flaws and lacked some relational skills. The good news is that he can change. The bad news is that both he and the churches wasted time and money. They both missed an opportunity to reveal the glory of God. Perhaps the music minister's problems go all the way back to the early days of his conversion. He may never have fully understood the pervasive work of salvation and the born again experience.

Self-Respect

The New Testament clearly states that we are to "glory in Christ Jesus, and put no confidence in the flesh" (Philippians 3:3). This means that we should not rely on our religious performance alone, as it pertains to our acceptance by God. We must instead rely on the substitutionary work done by Christ at Calvary. The apostle Paul declared, "Nothing good lives in me, that is, in my sinful nature" (Romans 7:18). Pride will prevent us from having the grace of God operative in our lives. In fact, the Lord promises to oppose the proud, as clearly stated in James 4:6 and 1 Peter 5. We must, however, have confidence in what Christ has done in us . . . and the potential and vision He has for us. This is actually humility, which attracts the grace and favor of God.

This is a good time to discuss a little theology. One of the clear messages of Scripture is that we are to exchange our unworthiness before God with the worthiness of Christ; therefore, we pray in Jesus' name. We come before God with an imputed righteousness because of Jesus' life of righteousness. We, who were unworthy, have become qualified "to share in the inheritance of the saints in the kingdom of light" (Colossians 1:12).

Charles and John Wesley, the fathers of the Methodist movement, struggled with the need to be saved based on grace alone. They had traveled to America to help others as missionaries, yet were confused about the true nature of faith in the power of Calvary. A Moravian, Peter Bohler, said this of them:

I traveled with the two brothers, John and Charles Wesley, from London to Oxford. The elder, John, is a good-natured man; he knew he did not properly believe on the Saviour, and was willing to be taught. . . . Of faith in Jesus, they have no other idea than the generality of people have. They justify themselves; and therefore they always take it for granted that they believe already, and try to prove their faith by their works, and thus so plague and torment themselves that they are at heart very miserable.[2]

John Wesley articulated his step of faith to rely on the power of God in salvation this way:

I was now thoroughly convinced; and, by the grace of God, I resolved to seek it unto the end: (1) By absolutely renouncing all dependence, in whole or in part, upon my own works or righteousness; on which I had grounded my hope of salvation, though I knew it not, from my youth up. (2) By adding to the constant use of all the other means of grace continual prayer for this very thing, justifying, saving faith, a full reliance on the blood of Christ shed for me; a trust in him as my Christ, as my sole justification, sanctification, and redemption.[3]

John passed on his fully marinated thoughts on salvation to the world in his sermon entitled *The Assurance of Salvation,* explaining the meaning of Romans 8:16: "The Spirit himself testifies with our spirit that we are God's children." The inner confidence that we are loved, accepted and forgiven by the Father is the result of two witnesses. First, the Holy Spirit who has come to live within us at the new birth assures us. Second, we know the promise of salvation in the Word of God. The requirement for salvation is that we repent and lay the whole weight of our trust on Christ's sacrifice alone for our salvation. Since we also know we have done what the Word prescribes, our own spirits bear witness to the fact that we have accepted the gift of salvation by faith. Wesley's words are brilliant, cogent and relevant to every generation.

Like Wesley, you must decide that your value is based on the fact that you have been adopted into the family of God with a specific purpose, according to Ephesians 2:10. God will never love you any more than He does at the moment of your conversion. You will never have to earn His approval because of specific tasks you perform.

Because of the worthiness of Christ you have worth before God. Ephesians 1:6 states that we received "grace, which he has freely given." The dusty pages of the King James Version declare that we have been "accepted in the beloved." This phrase, "accepted in the beloved," has been transforming for me. Once this truth has *really* gripped your heart, the Lord can put you in places of little or no prominence and you will still see your worth in His eyes. Perhaps this is why the sons of Korah declared in Psalm 84:10: "Better is one day in your courts than a thousand elsewhere; I would rather be a doorkeeper in the house of my God than dwell in the tents of the wicked." In other words, do not settle for the prestige of men at the expense of your commitment to the Lord. Now that takes self-esteem and faith! It is probably easier to do "good works for Christ" as a well-known evangelist than a parking lot attendant. Parking lot attendants who serve the Lord wholeheartedly may have more rewards in heaven than those graced to perform more visible duties.

There are those who have been born again, and the Spirit of Christ lives within them, assuring them that they are children of God. Because they have only a cursory understanding of the Word of God, however, there is no confident witness from their own spirits.

Usually they have never fully comprehended the heart of the Gospel—that they are saved by faith alone without contribution of their own merits. Wesley's message to them is that they must trust the authority of the Word instead of their feelings.

The Wesleys, as we noted earlier, had been confused about salvation and good works. Yet as they readjusted their theology and personal faith, they were a part of America's first Great Awakening. Thousands were saved and the entire nation was affected by the Wesleys, and others, who believed that God made them worthy by the blood of Jesus. My music minister friend is certainly saved, but he lacks the bold confidence in Calvary's work that our great champions of the faith enjoyed.

Putting Away Rejection

A sense of personal rejection separates us from people and is often difficult to rid ourselves of. You may think that you are rejected because you are not rich, powerful, beautiful or intelligent. I am not going to try to convince you that you really are rich, powerful, beautiful or intelligent, even though I know how Satan can distort a person's self-image. The problem may not be with the data but with your calculations. It is the way people come to their conclusions about relating to others that has caused them to be rejection-prone.

One picturesque way of looking at self-image is to visualize inner voices that are constantly whispering to you. How would these voices dress or carry themselves? Is there a big thug looking over your shoulder, telling you to be careful? Or is there a fatherly figure reassuring you with the words, "This defeat is not final." Many of us could actually put a face to these voices. We could see the faces of our mothers or fathers.

Many of us live out our lives in response to these inner voices. It is almost like being programmed. The Scripture is clear: "As a man thinketh in his heart, so is he" (Proverbs 23:7, KJV). Emotions of anxiety, pressure or fear may be simply the result of wrong programming. Let's renew our minds and strip the wrong voices of their power.

Think of these voices as being broadcast from three different radio channels. We can identify one channel as DBN (Devil's Broadcasting Network). The second channel is JBN (Jesus' Broadcasting Network). The third channel is SBN (Self's Broadcasting Network). If I tune into the wrong channel it often takes a few minutes to discern where I am.

The voice of DBN is easy to figure out. It tells you that you have missed it again and again. In fact, there is a tone of total condemnation. *Why try? You're not going to make it!* this voice declares.

Then there is the inner voice of JBN. This is, in fact, the work of the Holy Spirit. On the one hand, He assures us that by faith alone we are accepted and adopted into the family of God. On the other hand, He convicts of sin and shines light on things that are hidden in the dark closets of our lives. When the Holy Spirit is at work, He will usually confront problems with a sense of conviction and then restore the inner sense of adoption. It is possible for Him to withdraw from someone's life, but He rarely operates incessantly in judgment. The Holy Spirit's work does not leave us feeling in limbo or disconnected from God. In chapter 3, we discussed how the peace of God can function as an umpire in our lives. This peace that rules and abides is the result of the ministry of the Holy Spirit.

Third, there is SBN. It is the most difficult network to discern because it can fluctuate between sounding like the other two channels. A voice of self-condemnation that originates from deep within our own human spirits is the generator for SBN. Self-condemnation will always insist that we should have done better. No matter how glorious our achievements, working harder or transforming ourselves seems to be necessary. This feeling makes the young feel insecure because of their youth. At the same time, older men and women become unnerved by their maturity. The inability to simply enjoy God's blessings is a sign of this self-condemnation at work. Having high standards is a blessing that leads to excellence, but self-condemnation can create an oppressive weight around both your work and social lives. As a mature Christian, Paul said, "I have learned the secret of being content in any and every situation" (Philippians 4:12). He did not let self-condemnation steal his joy or peace as he journeyed through difficult seasons of life.

It is not always easy to sort out the source of all these inner whisperings. All of us are still learning the inner work of Christianity. Yet it is especially difficult to form a relationship with a person who has a broken spirit, low self-esteem or a weak understanding of the Gospel. People with these issues need to be propped up and reassured all the time. They will often misinterpret casual comments or constructive criticism as bashing. When the Spirit does indeed convict them of sin, they may even interpret it as being shunned by God. When the Spirit assures them, they can hardly believe it. There are many symptoms of self-condemnation. The list below may help you evaluate where you or friends may be buffeted. Those who are losing this battle are left to deal with the following issues:

- An absence of genuine love and acceptance
- Loneliness and fear of abandonment

- A diminished sense of value and a low self-esteem
- Insecurity and self-pity
- A struggle to meet the standards of performance-based relationships
- An attempt to compensate by boastfulness
- Lying about accomplishments and possessions
- Difficulty giving and receiving love
- A continual struggle with faith and forgiveness
- Deterioration of existing relationships
- Bitterness, resentment and isolation

There are many sources of self-condemnation, as we have already stated, but the road to healing is straight and clear. The most common cause of this spiritual condition may surprise you. It is typically unforgiveness and bitterness.

The Root of Bitterness

The writer of Hebrews issued this warning:

Make every effort to live in peace with all men and to be holy; without holiness no one will see the Lord. See to it that no one misses the grace of God and that no bitter root grows up to cause trouble and defile many.

Hebrews 12:14–15

Unforgiveness is an attitude of the heart that may well become a root of bitterness. Sometimes the things we deal with in the area of bitterness are not necessarily just tied to individual people. I remember one person in Corning, New York, with whom I spent a considerable amount of time. His problems revolved around his feelings toward rich people. He would verbally attack any person whom he felt had money. Asking him to specify what a particular individual had done would send him into a rage. A root of bitterness caused him to resent wealthy people, using the broadest stereotypes. Other people seethe with gender bias—hatred of men or women. This can be seen through sarcastic remarks, demeaning jokes or a generally suspicious demeanor.

Unresolved issues of emotional hurt and disappointment can be an open door for torment. Jesus told a story of a servant who had been forgiven an enormous debt by a gracious king. This unmerciful servant in turn went and demanded payment from his servant who owed him only one day's wages, and, because he could not pay, had him thrown into debtors' prison. Of course, the king heard about it and said: "Shouldn't you have had mercy on your fellow servant just as I had on you?" (Matthew 18:33). Jesus went on to say:

> In anger his master turned him over to the jailers to be tortured, until he should pay back all he owed. This is how my heavenly Father will treat each of you unless you forgive your brother from your heart.
>
> Matthew 18:34–35

Remember the reason people looked down upon those poorer than themselves? It was because they were unaware of their own poverty relative to God. In the same way, those who are bitter and unforgiving demonstrate they have lost sight of how much they have been forgiven. They do not extend grace because they have forgotten how much they need grace themselves.

Extracting a root of bitterness means you have to forgive people. That means releasing them from things that have actually been done, as well as from things done only in your imagination. Often that will not happen until you regain an appreciation of your own needs before God. Jesus said:

> Do not judge, or you too will be judged. For in the same way you judge others, you will be judged, and with the measure you use, it will be measured to you.
>
> Matthew 7:1–2

Some people are bitter at God Himself because of difficulties and disappointments. Jeremiah the prophet told God that he was angry with Him (see Jeremiah 20:7–18). He said something like: "I'm going out declaring prophecies, none of it's coming to pass, and the people are getting ready to stone me." Jeremiah 20:14–15 is almost unnerving as we listen to this great prophet:

> Cursed be the day I was born! May the day my mother bore me not be blessed! Cursed be the man who brought my father the news, who made him very glad, saying, "A child is born to you—a son!"

I am sure Jeremiah muttered to himself, "All I did was to say what You told me to say, and now look at the mess You've gotten me in."

Though what he prophesied did eventually come to pass, Jeremiah was very disillusioned at the time. After venting his frustrations to God, he accepted that God was in control and moved on by faith. We have to do the same thing: accept our assignment and walk with confidence and dignity. Unfortunately, many people allow these kinds of feelings to turn into bitterness that separates them from God.

Conclusion

Building upon a divinely inspired relationship is exciting and will always produce great fruit. If we can develop respect-filled relationships, we will be on our way to the next level of joy and meaning. Let me encourage you to do whatever you can to get out of relational ruts and to seize your moment.

But what about our self-image and overcoming feelings of rejection? Let's go back to the story of the music minister. Here is a biblical prescription for him that all of us can use: three easy steps to improve our journey.

First of all, he needs a heavy dose of patience. He is not going to renew his thinking over night, but he will grow in his awareness of the problem. The Bible says, "He who stands firm to the end will be saved" (Matthew 10:22). In this case I would rephrase that verse and say, "He who endures to the end shall be delivered and set free."

The second step the music minister and all of us must tackle is the problem of unforgiveness and bitterness. We must begin at the place of the most pain. Like putting antiseptic on a wound, dealing with forgiveness and removing bitterness may sting at first, but we must apply the Word in order to totally cleanse the wounds. Healing will only happen as the pain is acknowledged and dealt with. It may take a long time to see total deliverance, yet major burdens can be lifted immediately.

Third, the mercurial music minister needs to develop a consistent regimen of reading and applying the written Word of God. Many of us subtly search the Scriptures for encouragement instead of dealing with the issues that emerge. Learning new information and becoming enlightened is different from being transformed.

As we follow these three prescriptions, we will become a part of God's plan to cover the earth with His glory.

All three steps are necessary to achieve inner, personal transformation.

Transformation occurs as you ask for insight concerning an area that you need to change. Next, you should seek to activate God's power in that area of your life. Typically, this means you must start doing something or stop doing something. I am not speaking of heroic works. Just simple obedience to the clear mandate of Scripture. You must make a decision to change. True repentance is a decision that you back up with action. What is needed for many of us is a lifestyle of repentance, standing ready to deal with every new problem as it emerges. Repentance may seem like a wimpy response to God's Word, yet it is part of the reeducation process in the things of God. Repentance is sincerely acknowledging that your walk has not pleased God. It softens your heart and prepares you to receive the grace and strengthening of the Savior.

When you submit to God, He gives momentum to the growth in your life. James 4:7 says, "Submit yourselves, then, to God. Resist the devil, and he will flee from you." The enemies of your victory begin to flee. Once you decide to surrender to God in a particular area, your repentance and discipline will then cause the "devil to flee." Invisible barriers will suddenly be broken and you will begin to have internal joy and peace because of your decision. Eventually external barriers are also moved by the intervention of the Holy Spirit. James' words, "Resist the devil, and he will flee," are meant to be summary statements that describe a very intricate process.

Rapid transformation can occur as you follow the leading of the Holy Spirit. The Lord has a way of pinpointing the next most important issue in your life. As you continue to yield to the inward work of the Spirit, the sense of momentum increases. He decides the pace and tenor of our personal growth. David was very dependent upon the Spirit of God as he sought to grow. The New Living Translation of Psalm 27:8 best describes David's walk with God, "My heart has heard you say, 'Come and talk with me.' And my heart responds, 'Lord, I am coming.'" It will take an eternity to become like Christ, yet we have no choice but to pursue Christlikeness now. This is our ultimate goal.

7

Friendly Fire

The Difficult "Significant Others"

It is good to know what a man is, and also what the world takes him for. But you do not understand him until you have learnt how he understands himself.[1]

F. H. Bradley

Projecting military power effectively requires clear communications. That has always been true, whether orders are delivered using trumpets, signal flags or encrypted microwave radio transmissions.

An artillery officer, for example, needs to know exactly when and where his commanders want him to target the cannon fire. He does not need to be informed about everything his commander feels. But the artillery officer must be prepared to carry out his orders. To do that successfully, he needs accurate information.

Unfortunately, in the heat of battle, combatants can misinterpret the movements of friendly units or the

110

instructions from their chain of command. At that point, soldiers can become confused, concerned only with their own survival, and begin shooting at anything that moves, even their own troops. A tragic number of soldiers are mistakenly killed in every war by their own fellow soldiers. In a similar way, a lot of Christians have been wounded by friendly fire from their own brothers and sisters in Christ.

To survive a battle and win a war, the first thing you need to understand clearly is the nature of your relationships. The enemy, of course, will try to confuse the picture. Jesus once described Satan as "the father of all lies" (John 8:44). He is good at it and can tell very big lies. And so, on the Lord's side, the weapons of spiritual warfare are truth and the Word of God, and on the enemy's side, deception and propaganda. Satan is a master of using misunderstanding, misinterpretation and false information to wage war against the saints; consequently, the battleground of the unseen war is, for the most part, in your head.

Let me give you an example of how this battle against you might work. Just before writing my first book, I went through a trying season of introspection and isolation. Much of the personal crisis I faced resulted from decisions I had made in ministry three years before. Our church had purchased 87 beautiful acres of land in a prime area of the city. Although we had received "the Lord's price," due to the generosity of a wealthy developer, unfair politics and public misconceptions created an atmosphere of confusion both inside and outside the church. The pain I experienced came from the fact that I could not move forward to build a great church or sell the land. I was stuck in financial limbo for nearly five years.

These problems had repercussions. My church members are some of the most wonderful people in the world, but they were becoming discouraged. They blamed our predicament on a lack of wisdom on my part and the church leadership's lack of personal faith. As our morale sank, church growth and attendance leveled off. Some people complained about the praise and worship and even about my teaching style. I felt deserted and attacked. The problem with having a vision is that while you are looking at the horizon most people get frustrated just walking the pathway immediately before them. All of this was compounded by some nagging physical problems that just would not go away.

The stresses took their toll. For the first time, I wondered if I should make the transition into full-time itinerant ministry or join the staff of a university. Perhaps it was time to leave that local church that I loved so much. Those were dark days. A real battle was going on in my thoughts. The process of changing my outlook and moving forward with God was a significant one.

If you or someone you know is under tremendous personal pressure, this chapter may help you understand what is going on.

The Battle for Spiritual Understanding

Since the nature of our warfare is spiritual, understanding of the spiritual world is vitally important. We are exhorted to "be self-controlled and alert. Your enemy the devil prowls around like a roaring lion looking for someone to devour" (1 Peter 5:8). In the unseen battle, our weapons are far superior, our cause is just and the supreme Lord of the universe is there to ensure our ultimate victory. The problem, however, is that our warfare is on a different plane of reality. And so a lack of understanding of the spiritual world is the greatest hindrance to battlefield communications. When we misinterpret our Captain's communications or the actions of allied forces, it is possible that Christians will begin firing at each other or at the Captain Himself.

At first, relationships and warfare seem to be two very different things. It is important that we understand the dynamics of spiritual relationships because they are one of Satan's primary targets in spiritual warfare. His objective is to attack relationships and to separate us from God and from others. He is just like other predators who isolate their victims and then attack.

Our inability to forge, protect and maintain relationships is at the heart of many church and family problems. When there is conflict in the Body of Christ, it is often because Satan has exploited our lack of understanding in this area. He is at work whispering lies, dividing groups, isolating individuals and selecting easy targets.

When relationships are knit tightly together around the Lordship of Jesus Christ and people share a common cause of the Kingdom, Satan's schemes are usually ineffective. In my early days of pastoral ministry, a mentor of mine developed a group of elders who have served together for nearly twenty years. They were challenged, like any congregation, with rebellion, sin in the camp and many transitions. Yet they came out of all of this unscathed, while advancing the cause of Christ. This church became a great pattern to emulate. I wanted to develop church leadership that had friendship and unity at its core, versus technical proficiency alone. Very powerful work is done through organizations, which are also growing organisms. They are teams that truly love and serve one another; however, developing that kind of understanding and working relationship is a deliberate process, and you cannot develop that in five weeks or five months.

Likewise, we need to understand the dynamics of our relationship with God. The spiritual knowledge that supports our warfare is not what pagan spiritualists or the servants of Satan might think—a matter of spells, curses and incantations. No, what we need to know foremost about the spiritual world is the character of our Captain, the Person of God and how He deals with mankind. This knowledge and understanding of God is not so exclusive that only a few can ever possess it. That was what the first-century Gnostics asserted. Those who supposedly had this "special knowledge" about the spiritual world gained status. As you can imagine, that did not do much for harmony and unity in the Church. God has given each believer access to the knowledge of Himself. The apostle John writes:

> We know also that the Son of God has come and has given us understanding, so that we may know him who is true. And we are in him who is true—even in his Son Jesus Christ. He is the true God and eternal life.
>
> 1 John 5:20

It is true that the knowledge of God and His ways is not always apparent to the casual seeker; however, Jesus has given us His Spirit who will "guide you into all truth" (John 16:13).

Although most of us think that we have a basic understanding about God, it is only because we conceive of Him in our own image, assuming that He is like us. When things happen that we would never allow—if we were the lords of the universe—then our self-confidence descends into confusion and disillusionment. This trial of faith is usually a battle of understanding and perception. Perhaps we do not understand God's ways as well as we think we do.

At the heart of my personal trial was a misunderstanding about God. As I observed the various seasons of my life, I was unaware that God could make a winter season productive—*winter* symbolizing the time that all the externals wither and die. Leaves fall off the trees; fruit is not available. All the potential of the tree is seemingly shutdown and inoperative. In my ignorance of God's ways, I interpreted this as a sign of spiritual problems in my life. I knew that I was not being judged or punished by God, yet I could not explain the disconnect.

John 15:6 clearly says, "If anyone does not remain in me, he is like a branch that is thrown away and withers; such branches are picked up, thrown into the fire and burned." Jesus will never cast you away for bearing no fruit in winter.

It is true, of course, that Jesus cursed a fruitless fig tree (see Matthew 21:18–20; Mark 11:12–13), but He did so during a time when the tree's leaves indicated that green buds, often used for food by the Judean peasants, would be present. Although the true fruit of the fig tree would not actually form until a month or two later, Jesus could tell that this tree's lack of edible green buds meant that there would be no fruit that year. In all likelihood, the tree carried a systemic defect that would have kept it from fulfilling its purpose in God's creative order. He seemingly reversed the first blessings in Genesis, "be fruitful and multiply" (Genesis 1:22, 28), as a prophetic sign to Israel. God's chosen people had begun to shift their focus from God's purposes to their own agenda. They were, therefore, in danger of becoming fruitless as a result of their rebellion.

Most of us are not living in willful rebellion. A harsh personal winter will often produce a fabulous spring in the plan and purpose of God. These spring harvests will indeed bring glory to God. Paul commented on the veiled understanding we have while we abide on this side of eternity:

> Now we see but a poor reflection as in a mirror; then we shall see face to face. Now I know in part; then I shall know fully, even as I am fully known.
>
> 1 Corinthians 13:12

Lost on the Battlefield

The life of Job is a good example of how we must battle against misinterpretation and misunderstanding. Most Old Testament scholars consider the Book of Job to be the oldest book of the Bible. In these earliest of the divinely inspired writings, the nature and the motivation of our adversary is clearly revealed. In chapter 1, Satan comes into the presence of God to accuse Job. "He only serves you because things are going so well for him," Satan charges. Consequently, God allows Job to be tested but puts limits on what Satan can do. It was true in Old Testament times just as it is in the New:

> No temptation has seized you except what is common to man. And God is faithful; he will not let you be tempted beyond what you can bear. But when you are tempted, he will also provide a way out so that you can stand up under it.
>
> 1 Corinthians 10:13

At first glance, it would seem that Job was simply a pawn in a chess match between God and Satan; however, God cared nothing for Satan or his accusations. Neither does He act upon a dare. God allowed testing to bring Job into a deeper understanding and a deeper relationship with Himself. Job was a man on a journey toward understanding, and his chief obstacle was that he could not figure out what God was doing in his own life. He described his confusion and disillusionment in the following verses:

> He is not a man like me that I might answer him, that we might confront each other in court. If only there were someone to arbitrate between us, to lay his hand upon us both, someone to remove God's rod from me, so that his terror would frighten me no more. Then I would speak up without fear of him, but as it now stands with me, I cannot.
>
> Job 9:32–35

God approved of Job, declared him righteous and considered him someone special. In fact, Job's life had been filled with the blessings of obedience until Satan orchestrated the death of his children, financial ruin and sickness. Job thought he was cursed, rejected and punished by God. God was not chastening His servant, although his circumstances seemed unbearably hard. Job was interpreting his personal devastation through the lens of his own natural worldview. It was as if he wore glasses colored with the perceptions of the natural world, and God was not acting according to how Job thought He should. Job loved and trusted God, and he respected God's position. His problem and his challenge were that he could not understand the sudden turn in their relationship. It must have been similar to an abrupt change in your spouse's grooming style or personal tastes.

There was definitely a mental purging process taking place in Job's story. God allowed the circumstances to push Job beyond what his natural understanding could accept. For Job, this was uncharted territory and none of his previous maps was of any use. Job did not understand God and, in the passage above, he longed for a counselor—a sort of navigator to help him figure out where he was. His counselors did not help him much because all they knew was the information on the old maps. Some of their reference points no longer existed and new buildings were sitting where fields were supposed to be. Job was like a soldier lost on the battlefield. To get his bearings and determine his position relative to God, he had to start all over with a new understanding.

Because Job held onto his faith, even though he felt lost and abandoned, God Himself did eventually comfort him. People of all ages can experience the compound losses and confusion that Job did. Entering into a period of multiple calamities can be exceptionally devastating if we are also going through a major seasonal change in our lives. If these kinds of problems occurred during our teenage years or our late twenties, times when many of us set our career goals for life, the effect would be devastating.

Satan's strategy can even be debilitating to those in middle age. In this stage of life, we have the greatest combination of energy, experience and wisdom to advance the cause of Christ on the earth. Self-doubt teamed with physical changes and difficulties can cause many people in this age bracket to be temporarily or permanently derailed from God's purposes.

Women, for instance, might not have the same feeling about themselves as they recalculate what it means to be attractive, needed in their relationships or how they relate to their kids. Health issues, such as menopause or other age-related physical changes, often dampen a woman's outlook on life.

Fortunately, the Bible is constant even though we sense major change or instability in our lives. This is a period when Bible meditation or memorization would be very helpful. The Word of God will give a faithful reading of the changeless aspect of our lives. The Scriptures can become an anchor of hope in turbulent times.

Let me give you three important Bible passages. The first is Jeremiah 29:11–13:

> "For I know the plans I have for you," declares the LORD, "plans to prosper you and not to harm you, plans to give you hope and a future. Then you will call upon me and come and pray to me, and I will listen to you. You will seek me and find me when you seek me with all your heart."

The second passage is, "I can do everything through him who gives me strength" (Philippians 4:13). This passage will help you remember the grace of God that is available to you despite your current problems. The third passage, in seasons in which you feel as though your capacity is diminished, reminds you that Christ's ability is *not* abated. The Lord told Paul, "My grace is sufficient for you, for my power is made perfect in weakness" (2 Corinthians 12:9). As you search the Scriptures daily, there are many other passages that the Holy Spirit will highlight to build you up and strengthen you. It is important that we learn to mine these passages for all they are worth. The process of repeating them over and over again and praying over them until you see an inward breakthrough allows the Word of God to move from your head to your heart.

Understand that these passages are not for women alone. Men have many of the same problems women do as they move into midlife. In fact, Jed Diamond, author of *Male Menopause,* suggests that men have a similar physiological experience to women.[2] The prescription of memorizing the Word is just as applicable to men.

At root, the male midlife crisis is often an attempt to return to a former way of viewing oneself. Buying a sports car, changing jobs or even divorcing one's wife may be an attempt to retrieve a sense of virility, power or personal control.

For men of all ages, sexual prowess can be seen as a barometer of manliness that stretches far beyond the bedroom. Picking up on this dynamic among middle-aged men, the marketing teams for products like Viagra emphasize how much everyone will notice your return to control. These products serve more than just a biological function; they undergird a sense of self-worth. Dr. Ed Wheat, coauthor of the classic book *Intended for Pleasure*, says many male sexual problems are linked to emotions and attitudes, rather than physiological problems.[3] In my book *In-laws, Outlaws and the Functional Family*, I address a lot of questions about sexuality that will help men who are struggling in this area. Ironically, attitude and outlook are the major barriers that must be overcome by aging males.

Every chronological season of life has its purpose and its disappointments. In our youth-worshiping culture, it is hard to believe that the brightest, the best and the most beautiful also wrestle with self-doubt.

Younger people, for example, may be threatened by fears about their futures. I have noticed that men and women in their late twenties and early thirties often struggle with an inner desire to make a mark in career and business. Juggling the demands of jobs and family can often spread them too thin, leaving these young people with a concern about keeping up. Jeremiah describes such people like this:

If you have raced with men on foot and they have worn you out, how can you compete with horses? If you stumble in safe country, how will you manage in the thickets by the Jordan?

Jeremiah 12:5

Unnerved by newfound pressures of adulthood, many youthful divorces are the result of a desperate attempt to reconnect to happiness and a sense of freedom. Often the long-term problems of blended families, alimony payments and starting all over again only dig a deeper hole for those already overwhelmed. The answer is the same for younger people as for the middle-aged. We must draw heavily upon the grace of God. As we return to Job, let's keep these points of identification in mind.

Had Job allowed Satan and circumstances to steal his faith, he would have developed an entirely different perspective, perhaps one that would have led him off in the wrong direction—away from God and straight into the camp of the enemy. He had, of course, cried out to God to reveal Himself and to explain His lack of action. When God did speak to Job, it was in a most unusual dialogue that took the form of a series of questions. He said:

Who is this that darkens my counsel with words without knowledge? Brace yourself like a man; I will question you, and you shall answer me. Where were you when I laid the earth's foundation? Tell me, if you understand. Who marked off its dimensions? Surely you know! Who stretched a measuring line across it? On what were its footings set, or who laid its cornerstone?

Job 38:2–6

The Lord was demanding an answer. It was as if God were cross-examining Job's complaints about the way things were being handled like a lawyer in court. The bottom line was pretty clear: Maybe Job did not understand as much about God as he thought he did. The same goes for us, of course.

Breaking our mental constructs and paradigms is often harder than being set free from demonic forces. Neil Anderson's groundbreaking book *Victory over the Darkness* says this:

> The essence of the battle for the mind is the conflict between Plan A, living God's way by faith, and Plan B, living man's way by following the impulses of the world, the flesh and the devil. You may feel like you are the helpless victim in this battle, being slapped back and forth like a puck in a match between rival hockey teams. But you are anything but helpless. In fact, you are the one who determines the winner in every skirmish between Plan A and Plan B.[4]

Anderson implies that strength of character and willpower are needed in our battles. I have often wished that every battle would end quickly, as I shouted "in Jesus' name!" If only breaking the power of our paradigms were that easy, we would find ourselves instantly in new dimensions of fruitfulness in the things of God.

God often has to reveal our confusion before He gives us His answer. Similar to removing weeds from a garden, He works painstakingly to preserve and multiply only the seeds He has planted. This is a very important point. First Corinthians 14:33 says, "For God is not a God of disorder but of peace." He insists on removing hindrances to our understanding. This process is often inductive—we have to be ushered into a new truth by stumbling across specific things that point to our need for greater insight. No wonder Jesus declared, "Then you will know the truth, and the truth will set you free" (John 8:32). Thus, the Lord demanded that Job answer. He said to Job: "Will the one who contends with the Almighty correct him? Let him who accuses God answer him!" (Job 40:1–2). When Job did answer, he was contrite: "Then Job answered the LORD: 'I am unworthy—how can I reply to you?'" (Job 40:3–4).

It did not stop there. The next two chapters are filled with questions that God put to Job, demanding that, since he was so smart, he answer. In the last chapter of the book, Job finally says to the Lord:

> I know that you can do all things; no plan of yours can be thwarted. You asked, "Who is this that obscures my counsel without knowledge?" Surely I spoke of things I did not understand, things too wonderful for me to know. You said, "Listen now, and I will speak; I will question you, and you shall answer me." My ears had heard of you but now my eyes have seen you. Therefore I despise myself and repent in dust and ashes.
>
> Job 42:2–6

Why did Job have to repent? After all, Satan had attacked him! Like Eve in the Garden, Job had been lured into entertaining Satan's questions. These questions attacked the character of God. The word *repent* in Greek means "to turn around, to change our minds, to set a new direction." Job's repentance caused him to embrace the reality of God's faithfulness, despite his momentary tribulation. Years later, Paul came to the same conclusion Job did, saying, "For our light and momentary troubles are achieving for us an eternal glory that far outweighs them all" (2 Corinthians 4:17).

There are many barriers we have to overcome to understand the ways of God. Among them are our natural worldviews, emotional hurts and disappointments. We even have to defeat the whispering of Satan in our ears and the judgments of counselors who are confident that their easy answers explain everything. Job had to overcome all these issues and more.

There is nothing wrong with being temporarily confused about your predicament. Just don't stay there! Jesus seems to teach us that we must be resolute in our decision to obey before He shows His will. John 7:17 says, "If anyone chooses to do God's will, he will find out whether my teaching comes from God or whether I speak on my own." The basic training of every soldier of the Kingdom is learning to trust and obey, even when he does not see the big picture or know what his Captain has in mind. But when the lack of understanding turns into mistrust and accusation, then Satan's mission is accomplished. Job went from lack of understanding, to misinterpretation, to disillusionment—but never to verbal accusation. He refused to curse God, even though he had no idea what was going on.

Satan's temptation was to use Job's misunderstanding to get him to start firing away at God and at others. But Job was careful about targeting his weapon. He kept the safety on until he could get his bearings.

How many times have you seen someone lash out at God or at other people when he really did not understand what was going on? God honored Job's continuing commitment to faith and respect, even under a full-scale assault by the enemy. Satan did not care about Job having great possessions and taking things from him; that was only a means to an end. Satan's evil mission was to separate Job from God by means of misunderstanding, any way that he could create it.

The next time you are in the presence of God or reading His Word, He may confront *you* with questions. If He does, He may be trying to help you understand something about Himself. He may be erasing some of your own misperceptions. Like each of us, Job had a lot of questions for God, but he was asking about the wrong things. It is like trying to answer someone who asks, "How many good works must I perform to earn my way to heaven?" You cannot give a simple, direct answer to that question because it is based on a misunderstanding, a false premise that eternal life can indeed be earned by some amount of good works.

God helped Job see that his misinterpretation of events resulted from his misperception of the bigger picture—God Himself. The Lord wants to help you, too, especially when you are in the midst of a satanic attack. And the first step toward the doorway of deliverance may be settling on the right questions to ask.

So far in this chapter, we have examined some keys to understanding God's ways in a crisis. In the rest of the chapter, let's look at how to connect with others in their seasons of trouble.

Remember that we have many barriers to understanding God and others. Our own preconceptions and emotional responses color our communications.

In the Book of Job, several of his friends tried to counsel him but were very confused about what was going on in his life. Like Job himself, they simply tried to process his problems through the conceptual grid of their own understanding of God. All of us have our own ideas about how God moves. In fact, there are many people around the world who have created their own "religion," usually confused mixtures of half-understood passages from the Bible, along with non-Christian sources, such as Kahlil Gibran's *The Prophet*.

Folks who have formed their views about God outside of a clear, uncompromising Christian context are going to be confused. Their thoughts about God do not match what He says about Himself. They stumble in darkness, therefore, like someone who has entered a room without turning the lights on. They are in a room in which furnishings have been placed for their comfort and use. Yet since the light is out, the things intended for blessing actually wound or injure.

What is frustrating about this is that God will not turn on the lights for us by remote control. We must choose to follow the design of the room and manually turn on the light switch. The Bible says, "Your word is a lamp to my feet and a light for my path" (Psalm 119:105); therefore, we must read or listen to the Bible, submit to systematic biblical teaching and commit to prayer to turn on the lights. Christian books and study groups can add extra illumination in specific areas as well.

The problem with Job's friends was that they did not understand the ways of God and how He moved. This kind of "discernment" often comes as the Lord is promoting us to a new level. As God sovereignly begins to move us on, it may look like a severe trial at first. The key to grasping the misunderstanding of Job's friends begins with the darkness of their biblical concepts. Because they were lacking the big picture, they became an exasperating part of Job's trial.

Job's Comforters

Let's take a closer look at Job's friends and how they fit into the picture God is showing us. Their names were Eliphaz, Bildad and Zophar. In fact, they met together before they showed up at Job's place to discuss his situation. I am convinced that the Lord initiated their visit. Unfortunately, they were very ineffective in their mission of comfort. In the warfare against leaders, Satan delights in taking good motives and frustrating their intent by impatient and clumsy execution of the assignment. What should have been an opportunity for affirmation became an occasion for accusation. His three friends were genuinely concerned about Job, yet they made three mistakes: (1) They failed to help Job grieve; (2) they ministered information instead of comfort; and (3) they violated the principle of identification. Let me explain what these points mean. These three must be embraced as we minister to hurting people.

They Failed to Help Job Grieve

In Job's first trial (see Job 1:13–22), he lost his possessions, his children and the great majority of his servants. No parent expects to bury his own kids. In fact, the Bible says, "A good man leaves an inheritance for his children's children" (Proverbs 13:22). Job had been diligent to train his children to walk with God. By doing this, he had prepared a spiritual inheritance for them. In addition, he had cultivated tremendous lands and herds to pass on to them in the future. Job had been an excellent father who had prepared his descendants to achieve more with their lives than he had with his. A lifelong plan had suddenly gone awry.

As horrible as all of this was, Job's loss did not stop there. In the Middle East, many of the servants would have seemed like Job's extended family. In other words, he experienced his own personal 9/11. How devastating! Yet Job did not react to this loss in an appropriate way. The Bible does not record anything that looked like a normal grieving process. Job's response was simply to worship God. This may not have been as spiritual as it seemed. It may well have been a form of denial, an expression of shock, revealing Job's inability to wrap his mind and heart around these momentous disappointments.

His comforters arrived only after the second wave of calamities, which had to do with his physical health (see Job 2:2–10). Job had been afflicted with a skin disease that may have sounded to him like a diagnosis of inoperable cancer or even the dreaded AIDS virus to a patient today. His friends offered little in the way of sympathetic support. They did not know what to say. They deserved kudos for showing up, but they failed to lift his spirits or give Job a godly perspective. "Then they sat on the ground with him for seven days and seven nights. No one said a word to him, because they saw how great his suffering was" (Job 2:13).

At moments like these the content of our words is not as important as offering our friends our love and acceptance. A touch, a hug, a sympathetic smile will empower someone with the most limited vocabulary to speak as a messenger from God. God's comfort in seasons like this must often take on personal and human form. The grieving process that Job entered into would typically take one, two or more years for most people to get through. I remember when my father died. It took my mother the better part of five years to move on, yet she never remarried.

Job's friends missed the perfect moment to be used by God. They choked. They seem to have gotten angry at the circumstances. It was not fair in their thinking, and so their presence did little to relieve the pressure on Job.

After their first seven days, Job seemed to be even more depressed than ever. In fact, the very next verse says, "After this, Job opened his mouth and cursed the day of his birth" (Job 3:1).

They Ministered Information Instead of Comfort

Job was drowning in a sea of grief. His words reflected his inner turmoil. After hearing Job's curse on his own life, his friends broke their silence. Eliphaz seemed bound and determined to answer Job's major question: "Why is life given to a man whose way is hidden, whom God has hedged in?" (Job 3:23). Instead of identifying with the man's loss, Eliphaz essentially told Job to snap out of it.

Eliphaz did not understand that this was a cry for comfort and support. He was unprepared to let himself feel Job's pain any more deeply. His analytic response emotionally invalidated the seven days he and his friends had spent with Job. In other words, Eliphaz lacked the practical wisdom to be of help.

Some of the most caring men of our generation are beginning to learn that emotional identification is not a sign of weakness, but rather a higher level of true connection and encouragement. In the male culture of our day, men will typically take advice only from friends they trust. Eliphaz, no doubt, knew that he had that kind of relationship with Job, yet he missed the opportunity to move into a fatherly role of encouragement. One of the greatest roles men can play on earth is the role of father. Remember that fatherhood is one of the highest expressions of the nature and character of God Himself. The simple act of compassionate listening could have revealed to Job the Father's heart in ways that words could never have fully articulated.

With his flawed understanding, Eliphaz not only missed an opportunity to support Job but also misrepresented the character and intent of the Holy Spirit. He gave a speech, which he indirectly purported to be a spiritual revelation. His speech was based upon a very mystical experience he described in Job 4:13–22. He delivered this speech as though it were a prophecy, yet he did not have the benefit of Paul's writings, which declare that love must be the motive for the spiritual gifts (see 1 Corinthians 13). Eliphaz may have spoken out of fear for Job's future. He may have even wanted to make Job snap out of his depression, but his words were judgmental.

Since the Book of Job probably predates the rest of the Old Testament, Eliphaz had no scriptural frame of reference upon which to base his declaration. He simply blurted out the statement, "A spirit glided past my face, and the hair on my body stood on end" (Job 4:15). No wonder 1 John 4 says, "Dear friends, do not believe every spirit, but test the spirits to see whether they are from God, because many false prophets have gone out into the world." First Thessalonians 4:21 tells us, "Test everything. Hold on to the good." This spooky experience gave Eliphaz permission to shift from comfort to a tone of condemnation. This truly moves into the realm that Chuck Swindoll calls "theological voodoo" in *The Mystery of His Will.*[5]

At the end of Eliphaz's lengthy statement, Job could only respond by saying, "If only my anguish could be weighed, and all my misery be placed on the scales! It would outweigh the sand of the seas—no wonder my words have been impetuous" (Job 6:2–3). Eliphaz was the oldest, most mature of Job's friends, yet he had left Job even more discouraged than he was after their seven days of silence. If we analyze the words of Bildad and Zophar, Job's other friends, in depth, we would find the same kind of misunderstanding of both Job's needs and of the will of God. Suffice it to say that these men were unable to diagnose and respond to Job's needs. Their misdiagnosis stemmed from a major attitude problem that also plagues both men and women in the Church today. We quickly move into the realm of judgment instead of taking the time to identify personally with the trauma of those we are called to walk with.

They Violated the Principle of Identification

One of the first principles of ministry is empathy based upon identification. Pity is a very weak emotion that is expressed in a phrase my grandmother Naomi taught me as a child. She would often say, "There, but for the grace of God, go I." She meant that I should not look down on a handicapped or needy person because only God's goodness had prevented me from being worse off. "Big Momma," as we called her, was a true minister of compassion. She visited the sick, raised foster children and went out of her way to touch the hurting world around her. Conversely, we kids never really helped the people we pitied. I was even guilty at times of wondering what people had done to be so "messed up." This is exactly where Job's friends were.

True empathy would have moved Job's buddies to put themselves in his shoes. They would have attempted to serve him with an eye to easing his burdens. The first step for them may have been to remember their own disappointments or long-standing illnesses. Making a mental and emotional connection with people opens the door to viable personal ministry.

People can somehow detect when you do not respect their struggle. They wince at glib declarations made by the unaffected. But if they know how much you care, they can fully receive your love. They may even listen to your counsel. Paul summarizes the concept of identification in his second letter to the Corinthians:

[God] who comforts us in all our troubles, so that we can comfort those in any trouble with the comfort we ourselves have received from God. For just as the sufferings of Christ flow over into our lives, so also through Christ our comfort overflows. If we are distressed, it is for your comfort and salvation; if we are comforted, it is for your comfort, which produces in you patient endurance of the same sufferings we suffer.

2 Corinthians 1:4–6

Conclusion

If we believe that Jesus will lead us through our trials into victory, there is a positive side to being targeted by the enemy. The good side is that we will grow and become more useful to God and others around us.

Peter went through the same kind of struggle Job did. He endured a demonically instigated trial, yet God used Peter's growth and maturity to bless the entire Church. The New Living Translation sheds a little light on how Peter's trial affected his peers:

> Simon, Simon, Satan has asked to have all of you, to sift you like wheat. But I have pleaded in prayer for you, Simon, that your faith should not fail. So when you have repented and turned to me again, strengthen and build up your brothers.
>
> Luke 22:31–32

As we began this chapter, I talked about the dark period just before I began my first book. I did not realize that just like Job and Peter, the Lord was preparing me for greater ministry. At the time of this writing, I have finished the lion's share of four books. My trials have left me more dependent upon God than ever before. Despite satanic harassment, the Lord has helped me set new priorities for my personal life and ministry. I have entered into a season of tremendous favor and fruitfulness.

If you are going through a trial in your life, don't give up. Even if you have made major mistakes that have helped to create a crisis around you, Jesus wants to shine a light on your path through the Word.

8

The Code of Confrontation

Tough Love

All things are in God's hands and he doesn't want you for a sunbeam; He wants you for a soldier. He wants you to fight for truth and offer prayers for justice.[1]

Father Nick Gosnell

My brother-in-law grew up playing Army with friends and neighbors. During his childhood, military movies topped the charts. Gregory liked the idea of bravery and discipline, so he set his sights on the Marines and made it. This rebel-without-a-cause envisioned himself as a hero.

Recruiters promise young people the world. In many ways, they court and encourage potential enlisted people to consider all the advantages of a life lived in service to the nation. Gregory was beside himself when the recruiter's letter offered him entrance into the Marines. He had dreamed about being part of such an elite fighting group. It could not have been sweeter if Harvard and Yale had both admitted him to graduate school. To Gregory, God had smiled on him, yet everything changed dramatically at boot camp. Accolades turned to accusations and the real work of becoming a Marine began.

Another friend of mine arrived at an Army base dressed in his finest clothes. To his surprise the drill sergeant yelled at him, asking, "Where do you think you're going?" Then the sergeant snatched off his coat and threw it to the ground. "This is the Army," he screamed. My friend still remembers that incident vividly forty years later. Boot camp for most is grueling at best. If Dante's *Inferno* were written today, it would use military boot camp as a station in Purgatory. The leaders harp on every character flaw. They insist on compliance with every rule. There seems to be no other reason for the toughness other than to break the spirit of the recruit. Although there is some truth to this concept, the real reason for the toughness is that the services want their men and women to survive and to achieve their missions. This is tough love. The leaders are loving enough to confront.

In 1980 Goldie Hawn starred in a movie about a powder-puff private entitled *Private Benjamin*. A beautiful young socialite from Philadelphia became a widow after only six hours of marriage. In her grief, she stumbled upon the idea of joining the Army. The recruiter had actually led her to believe that people in the Army live in condos. He also intimated that European service was a real possibility for her. Her antics were humorous as she repeatedly attempted to explain to the authorities that she had signed up for a "different Army . . . the one with the condos in Europe." By the end of the movie, the Army had won out as she began to confront the lack of discipline and purpose in her life. Benjamin rose to the camp's challenge and served with distinction.

At various stages of my life, I have felt like a 240-pound Private Benjamin. I have, on occasion, awakened to the thought that I signed up for a "different army." Thankfully, when the Lord raises the bar of expectation, there is always a payoff.

Philippians 2:13 says, "For it is God who works in you to will and to act according to his good purpose." He often puts the desire to do a thing in us. Once we accept this call from God, He then gives us grace to do or perform the desire He puts in us. If we are not willing to confront ourselves with tough love because of character flaws or blind spots, the Lord will use others who see our potential to assist Him in a "boot camp" experience.

Some problems in people's lives are not simply a matter of personal destiny. Issues like sexual immorality, dishonest business dealings and divisiveness must be dealt with by leaders of local churches and ministries. Paul is clear about this as he writes:

> But now I am writing you that you must not associate with anyone who calls himself a brother but is sexually immoral or greedy, an idolater or a slanderer, a drunkard or a swindler. With such a man do not even eat.
>
> 1 Corinthians 5:11

Often the Church lacks the courage and strength of character to confront problems in Christ's love. Our confrontation must have restoration and redemption as its ultimate goal. Let me tell you a story that illustrates my point.

As I opened the door to my office one Wednesday, I was struck by the fine suit of clothes the man before me was wearing. The exquisite workmanship of his handmade suit seemed to scream money and influence. I was pleasantly surprised to learn that the distinguished gentleman was actually the senior minister of a church in our community. For the next twenty minutes, he told me a story of personal betrayal and adultery.

To sum it up, he stated that a man in our congregation, Robert (not his real name), had been having an affair with the pastor's wife. Robert was an up-and-coming lawyer who was raised in the South. Upon moving to the D.C. area to attend a prestigious law school, he had been taken in by this minister and his family; he literally boarded in their home. After graduating from law school, Robert stayed in contact with the minister and his wife. The dapperly dressed reverend looked at me with a mixture of anger and defiance, saying, "What are you going to do about it? I have heard that you are a man of integrity." My mouth hung open as I thought about the proper response.

How dare Robert betray this man, the Lord and us? I was not sure how Jesus would have handled this situation, but I was definitely not going to stand for this kind of outrageous behavior, so help me, God! It was clear to me that a "Matthew 18 approach" was necessary. This leader had confronted Robert and he had ignored the appeal. I would now help set up the second level of confrontation. Robert would have to repent or ultimately be removed from fellowship—sent out of the church.

As I pondered these things in my heart, I knew that the next few weeks would not be easy. Several private meetings with Robert and my elders found him unrepentant, denying involvement with the pastor's wife. I could not believe the audacity of this young man. I was about to learn one of the biggest lessons of my ministry.

I will return to this story later on in this chapter. First let me put a frame around the picture I have just painted for you. One of the important areas in every ongoing relationship is demonstrated affection and appreciation. Despite the high priority our marriages have in our lives, many of us are guilty of minimizing the need to say, "I love you," in ways our mates can really hear.

As we move beyond the home, expressing affection can be a lot more difficult to wrap our minds around. In this chapter, we will talk about expressing love to our comrades in the Lord's purposes. We need to create the kind of relationships that will make us all better and stronger. The hardest love to give or receive is the tough love of confrontation. Second, I will look at ways to fan the flames of our love for God, to truly express our love of Him.

Let's go to the Scripture for some answers. There are two Great Commandments found in the Old Testament. The first was the most quoted of all Scriptures, "Hear, O Israel: The LORD our God, the LORD is one. Love the LORD your God with all your heart and with all your soul and with all your strength" (Deuteronomy 6:4–5). This passage is called the "Shema," and every good Hebrew knew it. The second passage comes from the book of Leviticus: "Do not seek revenge or bear a grudge against one of your people, but love your neighbor as yourself. I am the LORD" (Leviticus 19:18).

The New Testament puts these commandments into perspective. A young man asked Jesus what he must do to inherit eternal life. Jesus replied:

> "Love the Lord your God with all your heart and with all your soul and with all your mind." This is the first and greatest commandment. And the second is like it: "Love your neighbor as yourself." All the Law and the Prophets hang on these two commandments.
>
> Matthew 22:37–40

These two commandments imply several things about relationships, church life and spiritual warfare.

First of all, the will of God, the purpose of the Church and the moral law of the universe were reduced by the Lawgiver Himself to these simplicities: Love God and love one another. You see that same kind of twofold moral code in the Ten Commandments. The first four commandments concern our relationships with God, and the last six our relationships with our neighbors.

There is so much discussion, debate and even division in the Church that is rooted in (1) the finer points of Christian ethics—should we or should we not dance, go to movies or fudge on our tax returns—and (2) the finer points of prophecy—what are we called to do and when will the world end. Many of these issues are actually a matter of personal conscience.

There seems to be a wide divergence of answers to the popular question, What would Jesus do? Some leaders are even asking, What would Jesus drive? Others have even gone so far as to ask the question, What would Jesus eat? Jesus, however, said that all of the law (the code of ethics) and the prophets (our prophetic vision) are summed up in the command to love God and to love one another. If you do those two things, everything else will work itself out.

Living the Love

There are two important things we need to recognize in the command to love our neighbors as ourselves. One is that love is not just a fuzzy feeling but an expression of covenant, of faith and of passion. And the other is that love is at the very foundation of God's character. Since the two Great Commandments are based on love, how we express love is a barometer of our walk with the Lord.

Real friends express love in practical ways, in both good times and in bad. Proverbs 17:17 says, "A friend loves at all times, and a brother is born for adversity." There are indeed times when it is not convenient, popular or comfortable to love our neighbors as ourselves. Usually people rally around those who are in trouble or who have suffered a great loss. Wordsworth wrote about a true friend, "Adversity brings him forth. He comes, as it were, out of the womb of calamity." However, a surer test of love and friendship is when a person is in "unpopular trouble." It is not uncommon in business settings for the ebb and flow of friendships to rise and fall with the tide of a person's position in the company. Everyone is a friend to the rising star headed for bigger and better things. When an employee is on the manager's black list, however, his old friends are suddenly too busy to talk.

The life and ministry of Jesus were characterized by practical love and care for those whose troubles made them outcasts. There was nothing faddish or trendy about reaching out to adulterers, Samaritans and Roman collaborators. He never hesitated to associate with the disenfranchised, the rejected and the unpopular. How much more should we stand with friends when they are in trouble!

A friend who "loves at all times," loves particularly in the absence of his friend. True friends show their loyalty by refusing to talk behind their friends' backs. I always want to speak about people in their absence just as I would in their presence. That is often very difficult because Satan tempts us constantly to change the tone and content of our conversation when a brother is absent. Our faithfulness in this area is one of the surest tests of friendship.

Love That Confronts

Taking it a step further, loving others as we love ourselves means that at times we will be required to confront one another with loving correction. Now we all have been around those who feel it is their mission in life to criticize, complain and point out everyone else's mistakes. That is not what I am talking about. That kind of person almost never approaches a person privately; it is always public or often behind the person's back. The apostle Paul wrote to Timothy about such people. "Besides, they get into the habit of being idle and going about from house to house. And not only do they become idlers, but also gossips and busybodies, saying things they ought not to" (1 Timothy 5:13). Busybodies and gossips stir up discontent and division. I agree with Paul; they need to get their minds on the Lord and keep their mouths shut about other people.

One barometer of Christian love is the willingness to take your concern before God in prayer, mention it to no one else and wait for the right time to talk about it with your brother or sister. Does this mean that we cannot talk frankly about a friend to our families or others who need to know? Certainly not! I can tastefully repeat things that have not been spoken to me in confidence. My motive may be to teach, to encourage or to warn. Just as Noah's sons, upon discovering their father's nakedness, chose to walk backward in order to cover him up (see Genesis 9:23), sin must be acknowledged and then we are to cover the shortcomings of our friends. I have been personally guilty of venting my frustrations about a friend with a team member. These angry outbursts can be easily misinterpreted by those who do not know us well. Talking to others within the parameters we have discussed takes courage.

There are many cases when it is right and appropriate to talk behind someone's back. Five occasions come to mind. First, when you are asked to give a professional recommendation. Second, when you are a parent, discussing your child's grades, advancement, etc. Third, when you are a supervisor who needs to talk about the poor performance of an employee in frank terms with your superiors. Fourth, when you are a ministry leader who needs to develop your team and deal with character problems of subordinates by conferring with peers. Fifth, when you are a counselor and appropriate sharing will assist someone in making biblically based decisions.

In healthy relationships we should tell our friends what we really think. We should not speak to a third party about things we have not shared with our friends. Dr. Henry Cloud and Dr. John Townsend confirm this approach in their groundbreaking book *Boundaries*.[2] Further, we say nothing with the intention of hurting or discrediting anyone.

It is really the spirit in which we communicate that establishes loyalty or disloyalty. All of us have friends we confide in, discussing personal matters. The royal law of love demands integrity of heart and a consistency of approach. Let's call it a personal honor ethic.

Mature Love

Another factor in the maturing process is the way the Church ministers to one another. From a Roman prison Paul wrote about how relationships with one another mature the Body.

Instead, speaking the truth in love, we will in all things grow up into him who is the Head, that is, Christ. From him the whole body, joined and held together by every supporting ligament, grows and builds itself up in love, as each part does its work.

Ephesians 4:15–16

A mature congregation is one that has learned corporately how to love one another and how to speak the truth to one another in a way governed by sincere love and loyalty. Each of us knows about areas in our lives that need correction, but there are also things that we do not see in ourselves. Brothers and sisters who confront each other privately and in love serve as mirrors for one another. They help us see things about ourselves we would never know any other way.

All of us have some rough edges that need to be sanded down. The Scriptures say, "As iron sharpens iron, so one man sharpens another" (Proverbs 27:17). True friends help us recognize and deal with the rough edges in our lives. It is tough to receive a point of personal correction from a friend; even tougher to give it. There is always the chance of being rejected. Yet a covenant brother or sister who is sincerely motivated for your good is hard to turn away. Proverbs also says, "Wounds from a friend can be trusted, but an enemy multiplies kisses" (Proverbs 27:6).

Christians who do not have the kind of covenant relationships where accountability and loving confrontation are regular, *nontraumatic* events go on for years with unresolved spiritual and personal issues. As the apostle said, speaking the truth to one another in love enables the Body to grow, mature and build itself up.

In my own life, I have found that very few people want to do it that way, but everyone wants others to treat him or her with that kind of respect. The command to love others as you do yourself has some very practical applications, as well as some significant challenges for those who practice merely the world's brand of friendship.

Responsibility for Confrontation

The closer the relationship we have with a person, the greater the responsibility we have to him or her. It is one thing to approach a brother politely about some minor social gaffe. That simply takes common courtesy. It is quite another thing to confront a brother about his offensive personality. The nature and depth of a relationship has a lot to do with what can or should be addressed. Let me suggest some general principles of confrontation.

God Watches Over Us All

It is the ministry of the Holy Spirit to convict us "of guilt in regard to sin and righteousness and judgment" (John 16:8). Pastors, other leaders and parents need to understand that though they always have the responsibility to correct those in their care, their words often have a limited effect. Wise leaders learn to pray first for the Holy Spirit to correct their church members or their children on the inside while they correct their outward behavior. You can force children to sit down on the outside, but only the Holy Spirit can convict them that they are still standing on the inside.

Parents Are Responsible for Discipline in the Home

There is so much public agonizing over problems among kids today—everything from underachievement to armed assaults on their schoolmates. Answers to questions about why and how these things can happen really are not as complicated as the experts make them out to be. I have discovered in counseling that when an answer to someone's personal problems becomes more and more complex, there is probably a simple answer that he or she has rejected.

Why are so many kids out of control today? Because of the breakdown of family discipline, mutual respect, unconditional love and togetherness. I am not trying to assign blame to anyone in particular (husbands, wives, culture or the law) because there is a lot to go around. Thousands of books have been written on parental discipline. Let me just say this:

Be controlled. Do not confront and discipline your child because you are angry and cannot stand it anymore.

Be fair. Kids are very keen to hypocrisy and injustice. Often they are not going to agree with you, but they have to know you are trying your hardest to be fair.

Be consistent. Teach your kids that punishment comes from breaking consistent rules. Arbitrary discipline makes you look like a dictator in their eyes.

Be aware. Effective discipline does not take place in a vacuum. The effectiveness of discipline depends on the atmosphere in which it takes place. It is the responsibility of parents to create that atmosphere at home.

With these principles clearly in place, we are ready to look at the problems of confrontation in the local church. Paul makes a bold assertion in his letter to his spiritual son Timothy: "If anyone does not know how to manage his own family, how can he take care of God's church?"

(1 Timothy 3:5). Undoubtedly he had concluded by previous leadership misfires that a lack of order in a leader's home exposes missing disciplinary skills. The personal lessons learned in parental correction can be a steppingstone to leadership development.

Team-building is also a skill that should be honed in the family before we practice it in church. We will never have an atmosphere where loving and loyal confrontation enables us all to grow up into maturity until we create that kind of environment in our homes. God's vision for the local church is that it becomes a place where three things happen: (1) people are genuinely concerned for each other's spiritual, emotional and physical welfare, (2) people abhor the idea of speaking vindictively behind another's back and (3) the motive of confrontation is always redemptive and never vengeful.

The Cost of Nonconfrontation

Jesus took the second Great Commandment very seriously. On numerous occasions throughout the gospels He addressed the subject of resentment and forgiveness. Over the years, I have been guilty of tolerating problems of abuse in a relationship for a long period of time. Eventually grace and graciousness ran out and these people began to grate on my nerves. This has led to my blowing up, telling someone off or withdrawing from the person altogether. It would have been better if I had confronted my troubled relationships before they became overwhelming and nonproductive.

One of the most difficult aspects of cultivating long-term relationships is developing relationships that are mutually beneficial. Significant relationships must be renegotiated. No self-respecting boss would pay an employee for simply showing up to work. Goals are established; reviews are given. In large corporations, this can be a formal process. In smaller companies, however, there is still an effective feedback system.

No army would ever survive if the soldiers were always wondering if they were doing what was expected of them. I have learned that I must be this clear in my personal communication. Further, I have learned that a biblical code of friendship means that I must be committed to the Kingdom's purpose. I must be willing to receive personal adjustments that will help "the team" I am part of. Similarly, my partners should be willing to receive suggestions that will help our team move forward.

Contrary to popular belief, the more closely we relate to others, the more often we will need to operate in the principles of forgiveness. This is part of God's personal growth plan for every believer. Even if someone is called to be an integral part of my destiny, we will still experience conflict and adjustment.

Guidelines for Confrontation

In Luke 17:3–5 we are commanded to forgive and show mercy. In the same breath, however, Jesus commanded us not to ignore offenses but to confront them. We are equally exhorted to be both diligent to confront and merciful to forgive. Along with the exhortation to confront, Jesus gave some practical guidelines:

> If your brother sins against you, go and show him his fault, just between the two of you. If he listens to you, you have won your brother over. But if he will not listen, take one or two others along, so that "every matter may be established by the testimony of two or three witnesses." If he refuses to listen to them, tell it to the church; and

if he refuses to listen even to the church, treat him as you would a pagan or a tax collector.

Matthew 18:15–17

First go in private. The Scriptures say that true love "covers a multitude of sins" (1 Peter 4:8). That does not mean you remain silent on such matters. It does mean that your motivation must be to deal with the problem without exposing a person publicly. This is contrary to human nature and the temptations of the evil one to talk about other people's shortcomings. Many so-called "prayer requests" are just religious forms of gossip. Go to your brother in private because you do not want to expose his sins any more than you would want someone to expose yours. Remember the second Great Commandment: Love your neighbor as yourself.

The second step is a little more challenging. "If he does not listen to you, take one or two more with you." That does not mean to get a group of people and gang up on a brother or sister. The spirit of the Lord's teaching implies that you should take along brothers or sisters who have the wisdom to mediate and bring reconciliation between two parties who disagree. Many times, especially in serious situations, this third party should be someone from the church's leadership team. As a last resort, the matter is brought before the church. Again, not as a heavy-handed measure, but to gain the wisdom and discernment of the corporate leadership.

Moving to this level seems tantamount to taking a case to the Supreme Court. In our legal system only cases with real merit should be appealed to a higher court. Most leaders in our generation believe that bringing a person before the entire church is the responsibility of the senior leadership of the church.

In many ways, dealing with egregious, overt sins is easier than muddling through the murky waters of

147

personal clashes. Attempting to get on good relational footing with my spouse, fellow ministry team members or someone at work may require much more wisdom than the three-step approach. I must understand that sinful patterns or character flaws must be confronted in my life and others. If I do not realign my attitudes and practices with the Scriptures, it will cause a breakdown in my relationships. Life would be simple if most of my relationship problems dealt with the clear and open sin of others, but traits like insensitivity and pride are more common booby traps that my friends and I fall into. Suffice it to say that learning to talk about the parameters of a relationship is the only way to readjust a relationship gone awry. Defining exactly what irritates me about a relationship is crucial. Hearing my comrades out as they struggle to come to common ground on issues, and offering my trust and respect, are also important. Relationships may change over time, but the important thing to remember is to keep the lines of communication open.

I want to discover the appropriate placement for every valued relationship. This takes time and commitment. Every little hiccup in a relationship does not have to be overanalyzed, questioned and repeatedly confronted. Some troubles need to be talked about quickly and then left to die of natural causes.

Haven't you had a person who was in your closest circle for a few years, but then moved to a cooler but still significant place? This all is part of the normal progression of things. What I want to avoid is the abandonment of relationships. I want to keep doors open to others.

Preparing for Confrontation and Reconciliation

Let's look at Paul's explanation of this process in Colossians 3:12–15:

Therefore, as God's chosen people, holy and dearly loved, clothe yourselves with compassion, kindness, humility, gentleness and patience. Bear with each other and forgive whatever grievances you may have against one another. Forgive as the Lord forgave you. And over all these virtues put on love, which binds them all together in perfect unity. Let the peace of Christ rule in your hearts, since as members of one body you were called to peace. And be thankful.

If a time comes when you must lovingly confront a wayward brother or sister, remember this acronym: *PRAY.* Each letter of the acrostic gives you some useful guidelines for the confrontation.

- Plan the meeting
- Rehearse the hard sayings
- Attitude check
- Yield to both God and man when appropriate

Let's look at each one of these letters in sequence. The letter *P* stands for Plan. The reason you must plan is that constructive conflict is very difficult. You must pick your battles wisely. A great question to ask yourself is this: Is the issue I am dealing with truly worth upsetting this relationship? You also want to define clearly the issues that you need to address. Sometimes delineating which one, of several interconnected issues, should be tackled first is very important. Finally, think about the timing of your discussions. It is essential for making the most out of a sticky situation.

The second letter of our acronym is *R. R* stands for Rehearse. There are always things that must be stated explicitly because they are easily confused or are emotionally charged for us personally. In either case, writing these sensitive issues down and practicing how to say them is important. In this way, you can make the most out of necessary confrontations. Like a doctor going into a difficult surgical procedure, you do not want to have to go back in a second time to clean things up.

The letter *A* stands for Attitude. It is so easy to make subtle assumptions about a person or process that can taint the outcome. Unresolved anger about the problem will make the confrontation unproductive. If I talk to someone about an offense in an offensive way, I may never get a clean resolution. I have to make sure that I have forgiven the person, even though I want to restructure the relationship or prevent future problems.

Jesus taught us that it is possible to overreact to a problem someone else has because we have not dealt with the same kind of problem in our own lives. Matthew 7:3–5 says:

> Why do you look at the speck of sawdust in your brother's eye and pay no attention to the plank in your own eye? How can you say to your brother, "Let me take the speck out of your eye," when all the time there is a plank in your own eye? You hypocrite, first take the plank out of your own eye, and then you will see clearly to remove the speck from your brother's eye.

This does not mean that we should engage in three years of counseling before we say something as simple as "Don't step on my toes again." It does imply that ongoing problems in close personal relationships may require growth on the part of everyone involved.

The letter *Y* stands for Yield. The Holy Spirit may redirect the tone and course of your confrontation. Praying for guidance is dangerous because you might just get it. The Holy Spirit always has a gracious way out of your problems.

What if you get into a confrontation and discover that you have your facts wrong? What if you have read unintended motives into your friend's actions? This is the time to yield, first to the Holy Spirit and second to your friend.

There may also be a way of solving a problem that did not occur to you in your planning, but that comes out as you discuss things with the person you are confronting. So you need to avoid being rigid as you pursue justice. All four of these letters in the acrostic *PRAY* were critical to our dilemma with Robert. (You will remember that Robert was the young attorney we talked about at the beginning of the chapter.) After several weeks of investigation, we found out that Robert had not done anything he was accused of. The pastor's wife finally divulged that her husband had been insanely jealous and physically abusive. She was even hospitalized after one of her husband's more severe episodes.

In his anger, the husband wanted to hurt Robert. I finally realized that everything had been blown out of proportion. When we went back to the pastor, he admitted to lying about Robert. He agreed to receive counseling and ministry himself. But what were we supposed to do about Robert?

I called a special meeting with him and the elders who had so faithfully met with him. The only thing I could do was to apologize profusely and let him know that we would set the record straight with everyone who knew about this. To all of our surprise, Robert simply agreed to forgive and forget. He even went so far as to say that he admired our willingness to look our problems in the face. Robert remained in the church and continued to grow in grace. In my way of thinking, both my elders' relationships with each other and our relationship with Robert grew dramatically. Good came out of the lie and the snare the devil attempted to use against us.

Conclusion

More often than not, people think of spiritual warfare in terms of cosmic struggles with wicked powers in the heavenlies. Not to diminish that in any way, we also need to realize that there are many practical, down-to-earth aspects to spiritual warfare. And one of those aspects is actively working to build and maintain relationships in the Body of Christ—even through loving confrontation, when necessary.

Part 3

The Warrior's Corporate Connections

9

Intelligence and Infiltration

Making the Right Contacts

Analysis is the core discipline in intelligence. As we face a new century that promises to be brutal and dense with human conflict, the ability to understand and anticipate our enemies (and difficult allies) will be the intelligence skill most in demand.[1]

Lieutenant-Colonel Ralph Peters

Accurate intelligence has paved the way for more military victories than bullets, bayonets or battalions of soldiers. During World War II, for example, German U-boats ruled the Atlantic shipping lanes, destroying hundreds of cargo vessels transporting supplies to England. Great Britain would have probably fallen to the Nazis except for the fact that Allied cryptographers were able to decipher codes that the Nazis thought were unbreakable. Instructions to U-boat commanders were no longer secret. With that information, the Allies could move decisively because they knew exactly what the Nazis were doing.

Perhaps one of the most interesting of these stories has to do with the 1944 invasion of Normandy. The Allies staged an elaborate ruse using fake troop encampments, wooden tank decoys, a flood of fabricated radio traffic and even the presence of General George S. Patton to deceive the enemy. The Germans were tricked into believing the Allied landing on D-day would be at Calais, a hundred and fifty miles away from the actual landing site at Normandy. Interestingly, the same intelligence tricks the U.S. used to confuse her foes, Saddam Hussein attempted during the Iraq war through the use of doubles.

In seasons of war, thousands of lives can be saved by the wise use of information and resources. As Christians, we desperately need to understand the importance of intelligence-gathering in the unseen spiritual war as well. Many Christians have a simplistic perspective on and approach to spiritual warfare. They are determined to give no place to the devil and would fight to the death against the onslaught of the evil hordes. They wonder, though, why he seemingly never attacks. They are unaware that Satan has been systematically infiltrating their lines and repositioning his forces for his strategic advantage. Faulty concepts about our warfare can leave us swinging at windmills like Don Quixote.

As Christians, we have access to both natural and supernatural intelligence. The Bible clearly states that "our struggle is not against flesh and blood" (Ephesians 6:12). Just before that verse, Paul explains that Satan has a strategic plan that he executes against each Christian. The schemes of the devil can be overthrown if we have the correct understanding of our battles. Although our goal is to seize territory for God, we are still in a war.

Our enemy is not asleep. He is lurking in the shadows secretly plotting attacks.

If any of us could predict future events with absolute certainty, we would be in a position to affect the destiny of the world. Both natural and spiritual intelligence is earnestly sought by those with dreams of world domination. Saddam Hussein believed that he was the reincarnation of King Nebuchadnezzar and was attempting to rebuild Babylon. I am sure that his hope was to tap into occult power.

It is said that Hitler sought to build his SS locations near the sites of ancient pagan altars. He apparently hoped to draw on supernatural strength that was evoked historically through human sacrifices and occult rituals. Hitler, like most other despots, wanted to both know and control the future.

When the legions of ancient Rome assaulted a heathen city, they offered lavish sacrifices to the local gods. They promised to serve the region's god more diligently than the historic inhabitants. This may be one of the reasons Rome encouraged the religions of conquered nations to continue. Rome's strategy was not just superstitious. She and other ancient nations sought supernatural support. The blockbuster hit *Gladiator* accurately depicts a Roman warrior's dependence on the supernatural. The lead character, Maximus, prayed often to his household gods and is seen as a moral man with a tremendous sense of duty and honor.

Christians should also be keenly aware of the spiritual dimension. While waging spiritual warfare, we should not limit our "reconnaissance" to the natural world. Knowledge that Hitler and the Caesars were unable to gain with witchcraft, superstition and sacrifice, we can obtain by the power of the Holy Spirit. The prophet Elisha's ministry is a case in point:

Now the king of Aram was at war with Israel. After conferring with his officers, he said, "I will set up my camp in such and such a place." The man of God sent word to the king of Israel: "Beware of passing that place, because the Arameans are going down there." So the king of Israel checked on the place indicated by the man of God. Time and again Elisha warned the king, so that he was on his guard in such places.

2 Kings 6:8–10

Warnings like that were frequent. So frequent, in fact, that the king of Aram suspected there was a spy among his top aids:

This enraged the king of Aram. He summoned his officers and demanded of them, "Will you not tell me which of us is on the side of the king of Israel?" "None of us, my lord the king," said one of his officers, "but Elisha, the prophet who is in Israel, tells the king of Israel the very words you speak in your bedroom."

2 Kings 6:11–12

Almost all the New Testament spiritual gifts can be seen in the life of Elisha, including the words of knowledge noted in these passages. Consequently, his ministry, including the manifestation of the gift of discernment, was a foreshadowing of the New Testament Church and the outpouring of the Spirit at Pentecost.

This chapter will explore the military concepts of intelligence and infiltration. We will look at the two major types of discernment available to every Christian. At the end of the day, we want to be like Elisha. If we can take the wind out of the enemy's sails and frustrate his plans, we will achieve our unique purpose. We do not have to be spiritual giants or prophets to win our battles. We do have to be teachable and choose to grow in the Kingdom's intelligence.

Two Categories of Discernment

There is a difference between the gift of distinguishing between spirits (see 1 Corinthians 12:10) and a discerning heart that is the fruit of a mature Christian life. Distinguishing between spirits is a free gift from God, whereas discernment is costly fruit. A residue of spiritual wisdom comes from rightly dividing the Word and walking with the Lord. This is what I call a discerning heart. Maturity is not simply a matter of how many years we have been saved. The writer of Hebrews refers to those "who by constant use have trained themselves to distinguish good from evil" (Hebrews 5:14). There is certainly a way to train our senses to distinguish the Lord's direction and plans for our lives. God wants to develop a discerning heart in us so that we are not ignorant of the schemes of our enemy.

A discerning heart is a constant source of direction and protection, while the manifestations of the Spirit occur sporadically. Many Christians like to specialize in one or the other type of guidance. We are typically either left-brained or right-brained. We are structured and analytic or intuitive and free-flowing. In truth, God wants to develop both dimensions in us.

The Greek word *phanerosis* is translated as "manifestation" and implies a fleeting demonstration. We should expect and believe for spiritual gifts to be manifested in our lives. But we need to be very careful about adopting an attitude that the gifts of the Spirit can be manifested on demand. If the Holy Spirit does not initiate and manifest the gift, then no one (even those through whom the gifts regularly operate) can conjure it up. This lack of "waiting on the Spirit" leads to presumption, mistakes and, in terms of spiritual warfare, bad intelligence.

What we know intuitively from a manifestation of the revelatory gifts is apart from calculated reasoning. It is a directive from the Holy Spirit that often comes without explanation when we have a specific or immediate need. If we are trying to witness to someone, for example, we might be given insight into his or her life. If a business deal is bait instead of a blessing, an inward alarm might go off inside us. The same can be said of the perfect job offer that really is not so perfect. In such cases, the Holy Spirit will just drop hidden insights into our hearts through the revelatory gifts. With that information in hand, a person with a discerning heart can then tailor what he should do or say.

The gift of distinguishing between spirits also gives us the ability to distinguish between the Holy Spirit, the human spirit and a demonic spirit. This is necessary as we receive advice from individuals or develop new relationships. It is important that we do not allow "Satan's moles" to infiltrate our personal inner circle.

Paul had to deal with these kinds of things. In Acts 16:16–17 he discerned a spirit of divination in a woman who followed the apostles crying out, "These men are servants of the Most High God, who are telling you the way to be saved." People in the region knew that she was a fortune-teller, and her endorsement of Paul and Silas may very well have opened the door to confusion about the doctrines of the early Church. On the other hand, there were probably many needy people who joined the Macedonian church because of this woman's celebrity status. God can sovereignly use everything to His advantage.

The Lord did not open Paul's eyes to the real nature of this woman's compliments early on because He wanted to set her free. Satan sent her to Paul, yet Jesus wanted to free this woman from her spiritual problems. Only Jesus knows how and when to set the tormented people around us free.

Thankfully, Paul did not have to understand everything that was going on. He simply needed to be an obedient servant of Christ. His writings show that this brilliant leader was both pragmatic and led by the Holy Spirit. So one day, as this woman was loudly extolling Paul and Silas, God let Paul hear a demonic edge in her voice that no one else heard.

The Greek word used here for crying is *krazo,* which means "to scream or to croak." I am sure Paul felt as though she was screaming. What triggered Paul to discern this spirit was that he was grieved inwardly. The word translated "grieve" is *diaponeo,* which means "to toil through in the context of worrying." It implies something that is boiling inside of you. If we do not pay attention to those unexplainable inner disturbances, we will march straight into an ambush laid by the enemy.

The ultimate proof of Paul's insight in Acts 16 was that a simple prayer set the woman free. Evidently the woman's deliverance was very noticeable as it resulted in her losing her soothsaying power.

Activating Spiritual Gifts

God has equipped the New Testament Church with intelligence-gathering capabilities that will enable us to discern the schemes of the enemy. Paul wrote to the Corinthians:

> There are different kinds of gifts, but the same Spirit. There are different kinds of service, but the same Lord. There are different kinds of working, but the same God works all of them in all men. . . . All these are the work

of one and the same Spirit, and he gives them to each one, just as he determines.

1 Corinthians 12:4–6, 11

The spiritual gifts were given for every arena of life, including the marketplace. Many strong believers have placed huge "No Trespassing" signs over certain areas of their lives. "I can prophesy in church but I cannot prophesy in the grocery store," they say. "I can receive insights from the Lord in a prayer meeting, but board meetings scare me," others declare.

Conversely, the Lord declares through Paul that spiritual gifts have been given to every Christian for his benefit and for the common good. I am glad that the Lord looks ahead, plans well and thinks of everything!

The gifts of the Spirit can be divided into three categories according to their functions:

- Revelation Gifts—words of wisdom, word of knowledge and distinguishing between spirits
- Vocal Gifts—tongues, interpretations of tongues and prophecy
- Power Gifts—faith, healing and the working of miracles

Primarily, it is the revelation gifts that are used by the Holy Spirit to reveal the schemes of the enemy. These gifts have been merchandized, abused and counterfeited. We have soothsayers on television acting like Old Testament prophets except that their so-called revelation comes from tarot cards or the voices of the dead. The Holy Spirit, however, gives gifts that will liberate and protect believers. Stay away from those who receive supernatural information in an unbiblical manner.

One of the most misunderstood revelation gifts is distinguishing between spirits. This gift helps us understand the primary spirit force in operation in a person's life. Let's say we are listening to someone share his feelings about a business decision or we are listening to a prophetic word in church. This gift will allow us to recognize whether this person is speaking under the influence of the Holy Spirit, the human spirit or a demonic spirit. We used an example of Paul ministering to a woman who had a spirit of divination earlier in this chapter. He discerned that the words of praise that were spoken about his ministry were energized by a demonic spirit in order to bring confusion and deception. I will give you some pointers on how to operate in the gift of discernment later in this chapter.

The Greek word translated as "gift" in 1 Corinthians 12 is *charisma*. According to Spiros Zodhiates, *charis* means "grace," and the suffix *ma* means "the result of."[2] *Charisma* is a gift resulting from grace or diverse manifestations of grace. Those grace-gifts are in contrast to divine rewards, given as a result of performance, dedication or spirituality.

In the parable of the talents (see Matthew 25), we find that people who are good stewards of God's resources may actually receive increases. The fearful man was disciplined because he buried his talent. His talent was ultimately taken away from him. The faithful steward with ten talents was blessed with more resources to invest. This is like a spiritual performance bonus. Spiritual gifts, however, are distributed in the Church to benefit the Body—not as merit badges. The Lord may warn a church not to buy a certain piece of land because of the hearing ear of one of its elders. We should not focus attention on the instrument God uses. The Church is full of imperfect people (including leaders), and the natural tendency is to formulate a kind of hierarchy of spirituality. With this kind of thinking, we disqualify ourselves as candidates for powerful gifts because we assume that they must be for special people.

These gifts function in different ways according to the instruments they flow through. The Holy Spirit rarely manifests Himself except through people, so when the gifts are expressed, they are almost always shaped by the earthly vessel. Further, we typically have to learn how to cooperate with the Spirit. No wonder Paul spent so much time in 1 Corinthians explaining how tongues, prophecy and revelation gifts work. Unfortunately, our traditions and preference for style can keep us from recognizing or receiving these varying expressions of the Holy Spirit.

Every person who attempts to move with the Spirit will experience some rejection as he matures in his gifting. Many people would not accept Jesus' teaching because He was a carpenter's son without formal theological training. He certainly did not meet their expectations of what the Messiah should be doing. By their estimation, Jesus was not even a contender. The personal background of Jesus, His disciples and the message of the Kingdom were all stumbling blocks to the Jews. This was no accident; it was a divine intention designed to veil the eyes of those who were prideful, self-righteous and self-exalting. God may also allow the eyes of people you are not called to serve to be veiled. Please do not be offended by those who do not receive you. Look for those who do.

If you do not understand that God uses people in different ways, you will begin judging spiritual manifestation by human prejudice and preference. I have been hoodwinked by people with perfect style, as well as by those with no style at all. On the one hand, personal charisma can be misinterpreted as spiritual anointing. An unusual presentation can be rejected categorically on the basis of style when, in fact, the message was inspired by the Holy Spirit.

Not all spiritual intelligence gathering is good information. Sometimes what is portrayed as a gift of discernment really is a critical, judgmental attitude toward others. When we fail to distinguish between the work of the Spirit and the work of the flesh, we again wind up hindering or quenching the Holy Spirit. We have to be able to carefully sort through the bits and pieces of "intelligence" coming in and decide what is valid, what is speculation and what is a ruse of the enemy.

Going Deeper

God does not always communicate in words. My personal experience with this manifestation has been that there will be a strange disturbance that I will sense deep within. It feels as though it is in the pit of my stomach, but it is not my stomach. It is just a deep troubling. I have this from time to time regarding situations, people and things I am going to do. This is like a red light telling me to stop and analyze what is going on. When I was growing up, my family loved to use the following phrase in this kind of situation: "There is something rotten in Denmark."

Discernment operates a second way in my life. Occasionally I will be talking with someone, and it is as though he or she begins to look like another person. I will meet someone, and he reminds me of someone I know well; let's call him John. I know Brother John, and I know his strengths and weaknesses. Over time I have found that God will do this to show me that John and this person are somehow connected. Usually it is the same weakness or the same gift in them both. What I am describing is not a spiritual form of prejudice or profiling that typecasts people. God is allowing me to see beneath the surface. Sometimes the gift is manifested simply to call me specifically to pray for someone. In other cases, this link between an honest-looking businessman and a crooked con man is a warning from God. This is a manifestation of the gift of distinguishing between spirits.

There have been times after individuals have sung in our church that I have gone to the music director and said, "Don't schedule that person to sing anymore for a while." It had nothing to do with the quality of the person's voice or presentation. There was just an inner discerning that is hard to explain, indicating that there were unresolved issues in that person that should take priority over public music ministry. God never shows me something like that to criticize a person. He is either trying to protect me, to show me how to help the person or both. Similar experiences are recorded in the New Testament:

> Philip, like Andrew and Peter, was from the town of Bethsaida. Philip found Nathanael and told him, "We have found the one Moses wrote about in the Law, and about whom the prophets also wrote—Jesus of Nazareth, the son of Joseph."
>
> "Nazareth! Can anything good come from there?" Nathanael asked.
>
> "Come and see," said Philip.
>
> When Jesus saw Nathanael approaching, he said of him, "Here is a true Israelite, in whom there is nothing false."
>
> "How do you know me?" Nathanael asked.
>
> Jesus answered, "I saw you while you were still under the fig tree before Philip called you."
>
> Then Nathanael declared, "Rabbi, you are the Son of God; you are the King of Israel."

Jesus said, "You believe because I told you I saw you under the fig tree. You shall see greater things than that." He then added, "I tell you the truth, you shall see heaven open, and the angels of God ascending and descending on the Son of Man."

John 1:44–51

Nathanael, responding to the Lord's call to discipleship, was skeptical and actually a little caustic. He said, "Can any good thing come from Nazareth?" Jesus, exercising the gift of discernment between spirits, understood his thoughts and his heart. He replied, "Here is a true Israelite, in whom there is nothing false." With the word of knowledge about what Nathanael had been doing (sitting under a fig tree) also came the discernment of that man's character.

Barnabas was the senior pastor of the church in Antioch. As such, he could see things that the apostle Paul could not. On their first missionary journey, John Mark deserted them and went back to Jerusalem. The two apostles had such a strong disagreement about the young disciple that they parted company (see Acts 15:36–40). There are people who are diamonds in the rough, who just need someone to invest in them. Paul ultimately came to see John Mark as being profitable for ministry (see 2 Timothy 4:11). He became a great leader in the Church, the author of one of the gospels and, according to early Church tradition, the bishop of the church in Alexandria. Interestingly, it was Barnabas who saw the potential in Paul when no one else saw it. Paul should have figured out that Barnabas had a real gift of discerning goodness in people.

Before Jesus selected His apostles, He went up a mountain and prayed all night. Afterward He made what would seem to be some strange choices. He picked a radical, a fisherman, a tax collector and a guy who was called "the knife" (*Iscariot*). There is a place for skills and personality testing, resumes and references; however, no one can see into the heart like the Holy Spirit. If you want to find great people to stand with you, look for the ones whom God has called, for with His calling God also supplies grace.

I have some wonderful friends from Arizona whom I believe were called of God to start a church there. I could also see that, while the grace of God was on their lives to start the church, they did not have the grace to be pastors and maintain the work. As catalysts, they were used mightily of God. Eventually they accepted the idea that they had genuine gifts, but they were not supposed to be involved as the senior leaders of America's next mega-church. If people try to do something that God has not called and graced them to do, they frustrate the people they are trying to serve and burn themselves out. Incorrect placement of gifted people has been a mistake that I have made over and over again. I love people. When I am with someone with potential I look past their flaws, as Barnabas did with John Mark. Unfortunately, our ministries and businesses need reliable people who are able to function with excellence today—not two years from now.

If we are going to build God's team, we need discernment. For example, I reserve the right to say yea or nay in all ministry-staffing decisions. Yet because of my personal blind spots, we rely on the collective discernment of our leadership. We also commit matters to prayer, giving place and opportunity for the manifestation of the gift of discernment.

The enemy is trying to infiltrate and destroy the Church today on all fronts. A few years ago, I was told of a church in the northeast where a practicing witch got into the children's ministry. She went in and supposedly started praying for kids to receive the Holy Ghost. What she was really doing was teaching them to chant various mantras. Eventually the church was totally destroyed because nobody with discernment was standing at the gate to prevent the infiltration of the enemy.

There have been too many cases in which childcare workers have molested children in churches. Even ordained ministers have committed the most heinous acts of pedophilia. Someone in these traumatized churches needs to know what is going on, and to pray about those they assign to work with children. The safest place in America for kids will be a church that has created procedures and policies using both natural and spiritual information to screen children's workers. Unfortunately, as powerful as the gift of distinguishing between spirits is, there are those who become over-reliant upon this gift and presumptuous. In such circumstances, spiritual workers can accuse people of intending to do crimes and thus tarnish a person's reputation.

Danger: Curves Ahead

Paul admonished the young church in Thessalonica about discerning the gifts when he wrote, "Quench not the Spirit. Despise not prophesyings. Prove all things; hold fast that which is good. Abstain from all appearance of evil" (1 Thessalonians 5:19–22, KJV). The New International Version reads, "Do not put out the Spirit's fire; do not treat prophecies with contempt. Test everything. Hold on to the good. Avoid every kind of evil." Here are several practical applications of this text:

- Do not receive anything as a revelation from God if it causes you to withdraw from the Body. Do not receive anything that does not deepen your love and compassion for your brothers and sisters in Christ.

Revelations that do not move us to compassion, intercession and understanding are suspect.

- Do not receive anything that increases pride in your life. Many Christian groups begin to wander away from the rest of the Body of Christ and into deception when they receive words declaring that they are *The Ones* whom God has chosen above all other Christians. Satan has no hesitation about deceiving us with religious encouragement. Religious pride is still just pride, and it is a stumbling block. Do not receive anything that begins to cultivate an unteachable spirit in you. Do not let your guard down; test everything.

- Depending on what kind of church you attend, either supernatural gifts or a discerning heart may be honored above the other. One can be exalted even to the exclusion of the other. I have seen the two sources of discernment compete with each other. People who manifest the gifts of wisdom and discernment do not trust what they consider to be worldly wisdom. People unaccustomed to spiritual gifts can become very skeptical and attempt to suppress those kinds of manifestations. We must give a place of honor in the Body of Christ to those with a discerning heart, not just the gift of discernment. This will focus our attention on the path toward spiritual maturity.

Discernment Based on the Written Word

The Word of God is the basis of all our decisions and judgments; consequently, we need to be skilled in our ability to understand and interpret it. The world is full of groups that appeal to the Bible as the basis for some strange and even bizarre beliefs. At issue are their

principles of biblical interpretation. Parables, prophecies and historical narratives all have principles and
boundaries for interpretation. For example, how do you
interpret an event in a historical narrative such as the
book of Acts? Was it a one-time event? Or will God act
in that way again? Or will He always act in that way?
Those are important questions because how historical
narratives are interpreted, particularly those in Acts,
serve as the primary dividing line between sects and
denominations of the Body of Christ.

I mentioned a verse from the book of Hebrews earlier.
In its fuller context it reads:

> We have much to say about this, but it is hard to explain
> because you are slow to learn. In fact, though by this
> time you ought to be teachers, you need someone to
> teach you the elementary truths of God's word all over
> again. You need milk, not solid food! Anyone who lives
> on milk, being still an infant, is not acquainted with the
> teaching about righteousness. But solid food is for the
> mature, who by constant use have trained themselves
> to distinguish good from evil.
>
> Hebrews 5:11–14

The Greek word *gumnazo,* translated here as *trained,*
means "to exercise naked." In order to mature before
God in discernment, we must let the Word of God work
in our inner being. God makes everything "naked" in
our lives as we submit to His Word.

The Greek word *diakrino,* translated here as *discern,*
means "to separate, distinguish, decide, judge or dis-
criminate." It comes from the root word *krino,* which
means "to separate, put asunder, to pick out, select or
choose."

In the last days, many will fall away from the faith,
and groups teaching false doctrines will be everywhere.

Biblical discernment comes by means of a discerning heart. Beware of those who teach unsound interpretations, claiming a personal word from God as their justification.

Four Chambers of a Discerning Heart

Many people are fascinated by spiritual gifts. In fact, they often tout the accurate operation of spiritual gifts as a sign of spiritual maturity. Actually, nothing could be further from the truth. The gifts of the Spirit are powerful yet fleeting. These gifts are safety mechanisms God uses in our lives as we are growing into maturity. Whenever there is a gap between your understanding of the Word and your current character development, God manifests His gifts to make you effective. The Lord wants to develop the enduring fruit of the Holy Spirit in our character. Character development is based upon a mature individual mastering four skills. Think of these skills as "chambers" of a discerning heart. To function correctly, the human heart must have all four of its chambers working effectively. Similarly, if someone is to walk in team discernment, all four chambers listed here must be fully operative.

Chamber 1: Personal and Moral Discernment

The apostle John wrote in his first epistle:

> As for you, the anointing you received from him remains in you, and you do not need anyone to teach you. But as his anointing teaches you about all things and as that anointing is real, not counterfeit—just as it has taught you, remain in him.
>
> 1 John 2:27

An old adage says that "a Scripture verse taken out of context becomes a pretext." Up to this point in the second chapter, John had been exhorting the Church to live above sin. His point here is not that we do not need teaching, rather no one needs to teach you the rudimentary principles of right and wrong because you already have an inward witness. Hebrews 10:16 states, "This is the covenant I will make with them after that time, says the Lord. I will put my laws in their hearts, and I will write them on their minds." In the New Covenant, the Church is not governed by an elaborate system of laws and regulations as in Old Testament times. The Holy Spirit living within you, as a believer, enables you to understand things from God's perspective and gives you the capacity for moral discernment. Whether or not you act on the discernment is another issue.

God has deposited the capacity for moral discernment in every person who has been born again by the Holy Spirit; however, this anointing that "will remain" in you can be polluted by philosophies and traditions of men. Paul wrote about this in his letter to the church in Colossae:

> See to it that no one takes you captive through hollow and deceptive philosophy, which depends on human tradition and the basic principles of this world rather than on Christ.
>
> Colossians 2:8

Let me share another theological principle with you. Many people have strange views about life, which they claim are based upon the Word of God. In many cases people think that they are drawing out the deeper truths of the Word, while, in fact, they may be reading their biases into the Scriptures. Scholars call the drawing out process "exegesis." This may involve the use of context, background, history and the definitions of the words in original or biblical languages. On the other hand, reading things into the passage is called "eisegesis." Sometimes when people declare strange doctrines, they are guilty of eisegesis. "Space travel is predicted in the Bible" or "My race will reign eternally supreme over inferior people groups" are erroneous conclusions based on a misunderstanding of the Word.

Thoughts in the mind can be the enemy of the Spirit in the heart. They also can be used as a defense mechanism against the conviction of the Holy Spirit. Rather than responding to the Spirit by acknowledging their sin and repenting, some people look for philosophies that excuse them from moral accountability. In an attempt to quench their own moral discernment, some people conclude that there is no God. If there is no God, then there is no absolute morality, and their conviction is only the result of social customs they can either accept or reject.

Chamber 2: Discernment of Lifestyles

Malachi 3:18 says, "And you will again see the distinction between the righteous and the wicked, between those who serve God and those who do not." Malachi says that there is going to come a day when people are going to be able to look at the righteous and the unrighteous and clearly see the fruit of their lives. God promises a reckoning day in which everything will come to light. In this present life, however, Jesus taught that we are to look at the lifestyles. In short, we discern true and false prophets by their fruit. They reveal themselves by the way they live.

Watch out for false prophets. They come to you in sheep's clothing, but inwardly they are ferocious wolves. By their

174

fruit you will recognize them. Do people pick grapes from thornbushes, or figs from thistles? Likewise every good tree bears good fruit, but a bad tree bears bad fruit. A good tree cannot bear bad fruit, and a bad tree cannot bear good fruit.

Matthew 7:15–18

We live in a world in which it has practically become a high crime to pass judgment on others, no matter what they do. This represents a universal rejection of absolute morality and of the Bible in particular. You have been given an anointing to discern right from wrong. Do not be intimidated by this absurd ethic of inclusiveness and thereby allow the anointing within you to be polluted.

Chamber 3: Discernment of Times and Seasons

Jesus rebuked the Pharisees for not being able to discern the signs of their times (see Matthew 16:3). If you can discern when it is going to rain, He questioned them, then why can't you understand the times? The implication is not only that this kind of discernment is within our reach, but that Jesus expects us to know how to interpret the times and seasons.

Our personal lives are molded by the purpose of God for the time in which we live. The Scriptures say, "For when David had served God's purpose in his own generation, he fell asleep; he was buried with his fathers and his body decayed" (Acts 13:36). Those who live in a different time relate to the purposes of God in a different way.

I believe we are in a season where God is realigning and reshaping governmental lines both in the Church and in the world. As we discussed earlier, first comes the natural, then the spiritual (see 1 Corinthians 15:45–49). This passage refers to the first man, Adam, as a foreshadowing of the man Jesus Christ. In the same way, events in the physical realm can be either a reflection or a foreshadowing of the purposes of God in the realms of the spirit.

The Bible says, "From one man he made every nation of men, that they should inhabit the whole earth; and he determined the times set for them and the exact places where they should live" (Acts 17:26). Often the realignment of geopolitical boundaries is like God blowing a trumpet. He is announcing a new season of His interaction with the people in these areas. There are cycles in the ebb and flow of rule and authority in the political arena. The natural realignment of governments around the world, particularly in the former Soviet bloc, has been almost unbelievable. A massive revival swept the Ukraine and Russia as a result of God's redefining geographic boundaries. There has been an economic shaking and a restructuring in America as well. America's financial boundaries are being redefined. This will also have spiritual implications for the nation.

Once we have understood the times and seasons on a grand scale, we can think about local issues that affect us all. We find that even churches and ministries go through seasonal cycles—harvest, pruning, cleansing, realignment, judgment and renewal.

As we stated in chapter 7, understanding God's objectives in each season will help us maximize our opportunities. We will also set realistic goals for ourselves and others.

Chamber 4: Discernment of the Holy from the Profane

Ezekiel arose as a prophet to God's people during their seventy years of captivity in Babylon. Despite their pagan surroundings, God desired to call His people back to a place of purity of faith. Ezekiel rebuked the priests for the way in which they compromised and allowed the Temple to be profaned. One group of priests, the sons of Zadok, had been faithful to both the spirit and the letter of the law. As a reward for their faithfulness Ezekiel prophesied:

> They are to teach my people the difference between the holy and the common and show them how to distinguish between the unclean and the clean. In any dispute, the priests are to serve as judges and decide it according to my ordinances. They are to keep my laws and my decrees for all my appointed feasts, and they are to keep my Sabbaths holy.
>
> Ezekiel 44:23–24

In each generation, leaders have had to apply Scripture to current events and issues that have never existed before. No matter how many rules and regulations exist, people will typically find a way to circumvent the spirit of the law to do as they please. With a little creative compromise and rationalization you can actually turn the intent of any law upside down. Beginning in the latter part of the twentieth century, we seemed to undergo a cultural transformation every decade. It takes a discerning heart to interpret and teach the Body of Christ how to live in the modern world, that is, the ability to distinguish between the elements of modern culture that are morally neutral and those that are profane in essence.

Conclusion

With regard to spiritual warfare, the most common application of the gift of distinguishing between spirits and a heart of discernment is to sound a warning when the enemy is spotted. God gives a sobering charge through Ezekiel to those who stand on the wall as watchmen:

> Son of man, speak to your countrymen and say to them: "When I bring the sword against a land, and the people of the land choose one of their men and make him their watchman, and he sees the sword coming against the land and blows the trumpet to warn the people, then if anyone hears the trumpet but does not take warning and the sword comes and takes his life, his blood will be on his own head. Since he heard the sound of the trumpet but did not take warning, his blood will be on his own head. If he had taken warning, he would have saved himself. But if the watchman sees the sword coming and does not blow the trumpet to warn the people and the sword comes and takes the life of one of them, that man will be taken away because of his sin, but I will hold the watchman accountable for his blood."
>
> Ezekiel 33:2–6

Discerning the movements and schemes of the enemy is serious business. People's spiritual and even physical lives can be at stake. Thank God that He has equipped us to be victorious in battle with the weapons of spiritual warfare. Our responsibility is to become skilled in using them.

Both the gifts and the fruit are designed to help us live "outside of the box." We will be more fulfilled than our non-Christian counterparts as we continue to learn how to draw upon the gifts the Lord has given us. Start seeking the power of God to lead you. The concepts of this chapter will help you begin. There is no substitute for investing the time it takes to learn how discernment will work in your life. It is a trial-and-error process. But know that, as you seek Him with all your heart, the Father is also seeking you.

10

Corporate Destiny

Esprit de Corps

There is no substitute for the spiritual, in war. Miracles must be wrought if victories are to be won, and to work miracles, men's hearts must needs be afire with self-sacrificing love for each other, for their units, for their division, and for their country.[1]

Major-General John A. Lejeune

Reggie White, famous all-pro defensive lineman, describes a winning attitude as moving into what he calls "the zone." In his mind, only fear and negative attitudes can break your flow once you are in the zone.

Entering the zone is something that great sports teams and crack military units have in common. Everyone knows his assignment, carries it out with vigor and lives with an awareness of purpose. When an entire organization enters the zone it is called *esprit de corps*.

Esprit de corps literally means "the spirit of the body." It implies camaraderie, community and dedication to a great cause. As Jesus said, "Greater love has no one than this, that he lay down his life for his friends. You are my friends if you do what I command" (John 15:13–14).

The greatest camaraderie, the greatest measure of *esprit de corps,* is found where people are willing to lay down their lives for one another. For that reason it is usually associated with the military where people have the potential to be committed to one another and to a great cause. Natural armies may abuse that commitment at times. By contrast, the beautiful thing about the Church's role as an army is that she is empowered by the Holy Spirit. This means that love, joy, peace, patience, kindness, goodness, faithfulness, gentleness and self-control (see Galatians 5:22) will ultimately reign.

The power of the corporate anointing that resides on a local church or ministry is designed by God to be a strength and encouragement to everyone who is truly committed. This chapter will help you understand three things: (1) why we need to work together in a hands-on way, (2) how corporate unity empowers individual believers and (3) how the corporate anointing works in the marketplace.

Every corner of our modern society is filled with people searching for personal significance and meaning. In his groundbreaking book *The Search for Significance,* Robert S. McGee tells us:

> The scriptures warn us that we live within a warfare that can destroy our faith, lower our self-esteem, and lead us into depression. . . . However, it seems that unsuspecting believers are the last to know this battle is occurring.[2]

Being part of a team that makes a difference can impart a sense of self-fulfillment. As we discussed earlier in this book, your self-esteem must be based on a bedrock view of your eternal salvation. But there is a legitimate place for spiritual ambition. Perhaps this is what Jesus was alluding to when He directed His followers to "seek first his kingdom and his righteousness" (Matthew 6:33). He juxtaposed making money as your primary objective and serving Christ. You cannot do both.

Some biblical scholars have gone so far as to say that the name "mammon" was the actual name of an eastern god of money. Adam Clarke, a great commentator from the eighteenth century, states: "The Hebrew *aman* means 'to trust, confide; because men are apt to trust in riches.' Mammon may therefore be considered anything a man confides in."[3] So the words "Ye cannot serve God and mammon" (Matthew 6:24, KJV) imply that the pursuit of personal wealth and goals alone will not allow us to fulfill the call of God upon our lives. We need to be part of God's army. We need the *esprit de corps* to make things happen. Our hearts must be truly ablaze with an intense desire to advance the purposes of Christ in the earth in a very personal way.

Seminars, retreats and small group encounters provide a measure of personal unity. But these programs alone will not produce the kind of *esprit de corps* that was prevalent in the early Church and in so many expressions of the Church since then. True Christian fellowship is not supposed to be an outing in which we serve fried chicken and potato salad. There has to be an inward work of the heart to produce a high level of connection and openness. It takes a corporate work of the Holy Spirit to empower and sustain genuine "koinonia." *Koinonia* is a Greek word that means "sharing in something with someone; a sharing; fellowship; communion." That only comes from a mutual commitment to a worthy cause. The Church is an army, not a volunteer fire department. If the Church does not understand and see herself as the army of God with a great cause and a greater Supreme Commander, she will never experience that deepest level of personal love and unity.

Pursuing True *Koinonia*

In his short epistle, Jude exhorted Christians to be as warriors fighting for a common cause. He wrote:

> Dear friends, although I was very eager to write to you about the salvation we share, I felt I had to write and urge you to *contend for the faith* that was once for all entrusted to the saints.
>
> Jude 3, emphasis added

Christians are to contend for the faith. That does not mean to simply battle over doctrine but to contend for the experience and the promises that our doctrine proclaims. In the early Church the community of believers expressed common faith and love in what has come to be known as a "love feast."

They would have a meal typically paid for by the more prosperous members of the congregation. The poor and the widowed would be fed by the financial contributions of those more prosperous. To the Church as a whole, this sharing was an expression of their communal love one for another. In other words, this feast was a way of saying that they were joined together in a bond of love, and as they ate together they experienced a corporate grace from God. The purpose of Communion was to recognize and remember what Jesus had done. The Scriptures say:

> A man ought to examine himself before he eats of the bread and drinks of the cup. For anyone who eats and

drinks without recognizing the body of the Lord eats and drinks judgment on himself. That is why many among you are weak and sick, and a number of you have fallen asleep. But if we judged ourselves, we would not come under judgment. When we are judged by the Lord, we are being disciplined so that we will not be condemned with the world.

1 Corinthians 11:28–31

The love feast, in my opinion, represents God's vision of us becoming a loving, caring community of faith. Healing and deliverance are a part of that vision. Jesus, however, is willing to do more than simply cast vision. He is willing to release His power. In Paul's day, those who did not "recognize the body of the Lord" and judge themselves were at times sickly, resulting in some extreme cases in death. This is a powerful and sobering concept. Christ's power that was supposed to be released through that time of Communion was hindered because they did not distinguish Jesus in both the membership and the Communion elements.

There are a lot of ways the Holy Spirit manifests Himself in a church, but the first and most important way is through relationships in the Body of Christ. Think about this for a minute. The outpouring of the Holy Spirit in the early Church was accompanied by a manifestation of the gifts. Paul wrote in his letter to the Corinthians that those gifts were distributed to various members according to the will of the Holy Spirit. I affirm without hesitation that the filling with the Spirit is evidenced by the gifts. But gifts like prophecy and miracles have been fought over for years.

While spectacular gifts are important, the apostle Paul felt that love was even more important. Billy Graham, in his classic book on the Holy Spirit, says this:

If . . . the greatest need of our world is to feel the effects of a spiritual awakening, the greatest need within the Christian Church throughout the world today is to experience the touch of the Holy Spirit, bringing true "revival" and "renewal" to the lives of countless Christians.[4]

Graham's point is very well-taken. He envisions a revival that touches our deepest levels. He understands the following concept: The greater the inward work, the greater the ultimate fruit. Shallow inner lives produce shallow Christians. Graham advocates a deep, internal revolution. The Holy Spirit's work, therefore, would have a very obvious impact on our lives.

In the last few years, many people have made trips to Florida, Canada or Argentina in search of revival. These pilgrimages were often life-changing for the sojourners. They frequently felt that a tangible grace was released into their lives. I do not want to question these experiences, but I wonder if we really know how to describe a true revival or move of God.

In my quest for more of God, I took a trip to Nigeria in December 2002 to visit The Redeemed Christian Church of God headquarters. Their annual convocation had an estimated attendance of more than seven million people. The sense of God's presence was electrifying. It was one of the highlights of my spiritual journey thus far. The reason I might call this movement a "revival" has to do with the personal relationships. If our internal relationships are transformed, we can move from that base to transform our community and society. In my thinking, the most amazing thing about the Nigerian experience was the corporate unity. In a country known for corruption and mass violence, an army of highly individualistic people had hung together and created a massive spiritual movement. As hard as it may be to believe, Nigerians may well be more independent than

Americans. I relished the fervent prayer, salvation experiences and mind-boggling healings that occurred. The Holy Spirit was truly at work.

In the New Testament Church, there were both spectacular manifestations of the Spirit and enduring graces that affected the way people related to one another and to the leadership:

> They devoted themselves to the apostles' teaching and to the fellowship, to the breaking of bread and to prayer. Everyone was filled with awe, and many wonders and miraculous signs were done by the apostles. All the believers were together and had everything in common. Selling their possessions and goods, they gave to anyone as he had need. Every day they continued to meet together in the temple courts. They broke bread in their homes and ate together with glad and sincere hearts, praising God and enjoying the favor of all the people. And the Lord added to their number daily those who were being saved.
>
> Acts 2:42–47

The evidence of the outpouring of the Spirit was unity, common vision, selflessness, personal sacrifice and recognition of God's authority and anointing. It was not distributed to a few but throughout the entire community. When people's attitudes create roadblocks to that kind of manifestation, they are opposing the plan of God and hindering an outpouring of the Spirit that could transform an entire city.

How Do We Access the Corporate Anointing?

I am convinced that it is impossible to live out the "one anothers" of the Bible without a church affiliation, whether it be a house church or a mega-church. We need the strength, integrity and purpose that relationships bring. We need the Holy Spirit to pour out the blessings of Acts 2. Listen to the words of verses 17–19:

> "In the last days," God says, "I will pour out my Spirit on all people. Your sons and daughters will prophesy, your young men will see visions, your old men will dream dreams. Even on my servants, both men and women, I will pour out my Spirit in those days, and they will prophesy. I will show wonders in the heaven above and signs on the earth below, blood and fire and billows of smoke."

The apostle Peter spoke those words, quoting the Old Testament prophet Joel. This inspiring message suggested that God's intention on the day of Pentecost was to pour out a corporate anointing on the one hundred and twenty people who remained in the Upper Room. They could have an impact on the city of Jerusalem, on Israel as a whole and on their generation. No person had to be left out of the Holy Spirit's power.

The primary anointing spoken of in this passage is prophetic. To prophesy simply means to speak for God. Jesus desperately wants us to speak to our world in His name. He is not limiting His realm of expression to prayer meetings, the Church or conventions. He wants us to invade businesses, politics, the arts and the entertainment field with this powerful anointing. Our personal ministry receives power as we are aligned with churches that are also aligned with God's purposes.

Our Local Churches Must Be Plugged In

When God empowers local church assemblies, it seems that there are certain universal callings. These callings are founded on the Great Commission, which commands us to teach all nations and make disciples (see Matthew 28:19–20). Yet there is a great diversity of method and emphasis that the Lord grants to individual churches. Our local church must be set free from the anchors of tradition for tradition's sake and "pet" ministries of elders or deacons. Our churches need to be set free to flow with the current of God. When you're connected with a church that is flowing with God, some of the corporate grace on that local church will rest upon you.

You and I will begin to find strength of spiritual expression in a specific area of blessing that God has ordained for our local church. If I attended Willow Creek Community Church in South Barrington, Illinois, I believe that a powerful evangelistic grace to reach "unchurched Harrys" would come upon my life. On the other hand, if I were part of Tommy Barnett's world-famous L.A. Dream Center, I would be out in the community, touching the "least of these" with passion and authority.

A great way to think about how God uses diversity in local churches is to think about a Baskin-Robbins ice cream store. People go to Baskin-Robbins because they have many different flavors of ice cream. Whatever the customer has an appetite for can be found within their doors. Baskin-Robbins would go out of business if they only carried chocolate, vanilla and strawberry. Although these three flavors are staples, they cannot be the only choices.

In the Kingdom of God, the Lord draws people the same way they are drawn to a Baskin-Robbins store. Our individual churches can be viewed as flavors of ice cream. God often allows new converts to choose the flavor that suits them. If all the flavors are represented, it serves a bigger purpose. The watermelon sherbet flavor has its purpose even though its sales may be low. It completes the range of options. It makes the store what it should be. In the big picture of God's Kingdom, He wants to use our uniqueness in addition to our similarities. Diversity is a part of God's plan. This analogy works for our entire Church and it works for us as individuals within our local churches. God wants to use our individuality to bless the church He plants us in.

Finding My Own Voice

Understand that as an individual in a local church you have a unique calling that must be lived out in five fields: (1) your job/vocation; (2) your hobbies/avocation; (3) your church involvement; (4) your community; and (5) your family.

Part of God's contribution to our individual success is the corporate anointing upon our home church. The unique blend of grace and authority given by God to your local church will bless every facet of your life. Here are a few Scripture passages that allude to the corporate anointing:

> They saw what seemed to be tongues of fire that separated and came to rest on each of them. All of them were filled with the Holy Spirit and began to speak in other tongues as the Spirit enabled them.
>
> Acts 2:3–4

> With great power the apostles continued to testify to the resurrection of the Lord Jesus, and much grace was upon them all.
>
> Acts 4:33

> "After that you will go to Gibeah of God, where there is a Philistine outpost. As you approach the town, you will meet a procession of prophets coming down from the high place with lyres, tambourines, flutes and harps

being played before them, and they will be prophesying. The Spirit of the LORD will come upon you in power, and you will prophesy with them; and you will be changed into a different person."

1 Samuel 10:5–6

The anointing of God is not just for preachers or ministers. God's empowering is for the entire Body of Christ. The best way to show you how this works is to take you back to the story of Moses at a very vulnerable point in his life. In Numbers 11 the mixed multitude complained greatly about their hardships and their journey with Moses and God. This corporate dissatisfaction angered God and caused Him to send a fire among the people. Only Moses' prayers were able to put the fire out.

Immediately after this crisis, Moses heard a second wave of murmuring rise up among the people about their food (see Numbers 11:4–5). Moses became disheartened because of the ceaseless complaints. He even asked God to kill him if he had to live under that pressure permanently. The Lord never intended one man to carry the weight of an entire church. He does often choose one heart to be the spiritual nursery in which He incubates the vision and anointing for an entire church, though. As Moses prayed about these things, the Lord told him to gather elders who would be able to help him lead:

The LORD said to Moses: "Bring me seventy of Israel's elders who are known to you as leaders and officials among the people. Have them come to the Tent of Meeting, that they may stand there with you. I will come down and speak with you there, and I will take of the Spirit that is on you and put the Spirit on them. They will help you carry the burden of the people so that you will not have to carry it alone."

Numbers 11:16–17

Moses' request for help was answered by God taking the very same anointing that was upon his life and sharing it with seventy elders. When the Holy Spirit rested upon them, they began to prophesy (see Numbers 11:25). This meant that Moses' prophetic mantle had actually been extended to them. They were not to do the work of caring for their nation *instead* of Moses. They were being commissioned to work along *with* Moses.

The most amazing aspect of this story is that two men, Eldad and Medad, had not come to the empowerment service that God instructed Moses to hold. Nonetheless these two men, who were joined in heart, began to prophesy at the same time in a remote location. This proves that there is no distance in the anointing. If we are connected with our leaders, we can move in the corporate anointing upon our church in the marketplace, in the courtroom or wherever we have been assigned.

In an ideal world God wants to use us as individuals who operate under a corporate anointing. You have unique talents and abilities that God has given. Let's return to the reference we made in the last chapter about the parable of the talents from Matthew 25:14–30. In this teaching, Jesus helps us understand that when God gives talents to people, there actually is a twofold work of grace operating in each of our lives. A close examination of Matthew 25:15 points this out: "To one he gave five talents of money, to another two talents, and to another one talent, each according to his ability. Then he went on his journey."

First, the talents were given according to the person's ability. This means that before we were born certain natural talents and acumen were given. We have not all been created with the same kind or measure of natural gifts.

Second, in His mercy, God gifts me with "talents" (in the Bible, this was a monetary investment), based on my ability to handle His gift. As I have read and reread this parable, I have come to the conclusion that God plans ahead. He gives everything I need to be successful before He gives me the money, influence or opportunity that He has ordained for a special season of blessing in my life.

God never gives us more than we can bear (see 1 Corinthians 10:13), but poor choices can frustrate His grace. I must be committed to prayerfully prioritizing my time and investing the gifts God gives me (for *His* glory) in the five major arenas of my life.

In my local church, God has made the purpose of corporate anointing real to me time and time again. The corporate anointing is one of the factors designed to catapult you into your unique calling and destiny. It matters, therefore, who disciples you and what local church you connect with. The best example of this is the life of one of my spiritual sons, Alvin Smith. In his journey to discern God's will, he spent nearly a year as a pastor. Frustrated by that experience, he felt called to return to the secular marketplace. Alvin decided that his gifting was more prophetic than pastoral.

When he returned to the District of Columbia metro area, he gave himself to prayer and reconnected with our local church. Alvin had to struggle with feelings of failure and even bitterness. Although he is a powerful communicator of God's Word, Alvin recognized that his success had to be based upon obedience to a special calling. He returned to his old company under the cloud of being over-committed spiritually. As he was given assignments at work, much to Alvin's surprise, the prophetic gift began to operate on his job. He instinctively knew what to do to increase profits, eliminate waste and improve productivity. His personal diligence made his company hundreds of thousands of dollars in profit. One of his major accomplishments was saving an account worth three or four million dollars annually for the company. He never used the phrase *Thus saith the Lord . . .* to preface his suggestions or insights on the job. He simply walked in the principle that "wisdom is justified of her children" (Matthew 11:19, KJV).

After just three years back with his company, his salary quadrupled. Everyone in his company knows that he is a Christian. He has been used by God to lead many people to Christ. Two notable cases come to mind.

One of the foremen at Alvin's job was in great emotional turmoil. Everyone was concerned about the foreman's well-being. Knowing that he was a preacher, fellow workers asked Alvin to intervene. Members of a cult group had also been asked for their help. Alvin knew that he had to beat the cult members to the punch. Thank God he did! He prayed the sinner's prayer with this gentleman, and helped him sort through many emotional issues. After this incident, one of the cult members watched Alvin for over a year. He was intrigued by Alvin's consistent lifestyle. Then one day he made the step of faith to repent and receive Jesus Christ as his Lord and Savior.

On another occasion Alvin got a call from a fellow worker. He heard a gravelly voice on the other end of the phone say, "Alvin, I need to see you." The man was going through a divorce and did not know how to handle it. He was so overwrought that he wept convulsively as he told Alvin his story. The custody battle that he was in made him afraid that he would lose everything, including the right to see his children. Alvin led him to Christ on a construction site in front of other workers. God turned this man's life around and straightened out the ugly custody battle. Years later, this gentleman is still serving Christ and his local church.

Conclusion

The Lord wants to use every believer for His glory. We have not been wired by God to work alone. We need fellowship, inspiration and teamwork.

I am determined to live by the principles outlined in this chapter. Is it a lot of work? You bet, but there are great rewards!

11

Command and Commanders

Mobilizing the Body

To know how to command obedience is a very different thing from making men obey. Obedience is not the
product of fear, but of understanding, and understanding
is based on knowledge.[1]

Brigadier-General S. L. A. Marshall

A friend of mine flew "shotgun" on a medical heli-
copter in Vietnam. They landed in remote places and
picked up the dying and wounded. Under heavy fire,
they sometimes had to decide who was rescued and
who was left behind. His team did not play God. They
simply had a unique opportunity to intervene in the
name of God.

As a military medic, it may be easier to view yourself
as a part of the answer—a force for good in an unpleas-
ant situation. Other military leaders do not have the
luxury of such clear focus. It has to be different if your

goal is less tangible. Our recent wars, like the one in Iraq, have had blurred boundaries. A soldier's opponents are not wearing the colors of an enemy army. Standing in some remote Middle-Eastern village, U.S. soldiers must decide who is a threat and who is not. There is an obscure line of demarcation between risk, reward or reversal.

During the Iraq war, CBS News reporters Byron Pitts, Jim Axelrod and Mark Strassman were embedded with a U.S. battalion. Byron Pitts was impressed by a 31-year old captain from Harrisburg, Pennsylvania, who was in charge of Lima Company as they came under attack on the streets of Baghdad. His calm directions that day actually saved innocent lives. As Pitts recalls:

> There was one point where one of the young corporals said, "Sir, we spotted where the fire is coming from. There are three people, let me take the shot."
>
> The captain said, "Have you identified their weapons?"
>
> The corporal admitted, "No, sir."
>
> The captain reaffirmed, "Don't take the shot until you can confirm the weapon."
>
> Even though the corporal kept pushing, the captain wouldn't allow anyone to return fire. Moments passed and they saw three heads bobbing up and down. The Marines all assumed that these were the enemy. Within moments, however, a man, his wife, and daughter stood up. Because this captain made the right call, three people are alive today.
>
> We talked later about it. I said, "How were you so calm?"
>
> He said, "Byron, trust me, on the inside I was as frightened as anyone. But I had to keep my men calm. And they looked to me for direction."
>
> That was a wonderful moment.[2]

The young captain from Harrisburg made a very wise decision, yet it could have turned out badly for him. War is a dangerous enterprise. In several other situations, senseless deaths of American troops occurred as they sought to help Iraqi children. Good intentions do not always make up for bad choices.

No one, including army officers, makes the right decision 100 percent of the time. Despite any leader's limitations, there is an obvious chain of command in war. There has to be.

Simply knowing that people on both sides will die because of a directive you make will sober up the most irreverent of us. The heavy responsibility of ordering men into combat seems unimaginable to most of us. CNN and other news agencies made the grim realities of war very clear in the Iraq war. Great generals from past wars were not always right. No one is. But they saw the big picture and made the big-picture decisions well. They chose to fight the right battle at the right time for the right reasons. Yet all of our heroes were human. They all had clay feet.

Spiritual leaders are often no more insightful than natural leaders. It is good to know that God Himself has ordained levels of human authority. Flawed individuals serve as His representatives. Both leaders and followers must exercise a high degree of faith in God as they work together. In recent years, the Church has often forgotten that she is at war. Moral scandals of great magnitude have plagued every branch of the Church. When leaders lose their moral compass, they begin to drift off course. Leadership failures have blackened the eye of the Church like no other problem. Both Protestants and Catholics need to reevaluate how they view earthly authority in Christ's army. Obviously checks, balances, boards and structure are needed to keep the organized Church moving forward. Despite all this we still need spiritual leaders. It is vital to understand and acknowledge this because there can be no unity without leadership.

The Lord seems to have arbitrarily (from our perspective) chosen senior leaders and their teams to spearhead His work. In Moses' day, the entire nation followed the cloud of God (see Exodus 13:20). As they moved through the wilderness there was a sequence and an order in which they moved. The cloud represented the presence of God protecting them as a group. They had to move when God said to move and stop when God said to stop. And they had to remain together. God did not need Moses' personal strength to defeat the enemies of His people. He needed Moses' obedience to His direction. No wonder Moses said in Numbers 10:35, "Rise up, O LORD! May your enemies be scattered; may your foes flee before you."

David, a great military leader, repeats the words of Moses in Psalm 68:1, "Let God arise, let his enemies be scattered" (KJV). Both Moses and David were gifted with unusual natural talent and ability. Their unique callings placed them in a position of great need. If they were to be successful, it would take the hand of God resting upon them. They were responsible to God for millions of people. God's ability alone made both of these great leaders effective. No wonder the Scriptures record their common cry, "Let God arise, let His enemies be scattered!"

Every individual must see himself as a leader called by God. He has a sphere of influence that God expects him to steward. Henry and Tom Blackaby say in *The Man God Uses*, "If you take responsibility for your relationship with God, it will impact your marriage, children, neighbors and others. When God makes a covenant with a man, it traditionally includes his descendants as well."[3] The Kingdom of God moves forward as interconnected leaders learn to defer to one another.

The purpose of this chapter is not to encourage blind obedience to earthly leaders. My goal is to paint a clear picture of how the Lord intended authority to function in the Church. Further, I will expose several subtle philosophies that prevent the corporate anointing from functioning powerfully in our churches. The Church's natural and spiritual resources are so massive that we could change the face of any nation if we could simply unite under the leadership of our Commander in Chief.

Unfortunately, most of our efforts to unite the Church start at the global level. We want an entire city to unite and move together. What if the Lord desires to bring us together from the bottom up? What if He wants more unity within each local church? If so, serving faithfully as an usher would be a step to change our world. Further, if the usher-by-evening served as a bank-president-by-day, we would be able to infiltrate the financial community. Eventually we could have good people committing strategic acts of kindness in every strata of society.

The Blessing of God Commanded

The very core of each local church's effectiveness is based upon two powerful principles. The first principle involves the God-given role of the Church. A church has delegated authority in the earth. Jesus said that the gates of hell would not prevail against the Church. In Matthew 16:19, He goes on to declare, "I will give you the keys of the kingdom of heaven; whatever you bind on earth will be bound in heaven, and whatever you loose on earth will be loosed in heaven."

The Church's privilege of binding and loosing is intended to advance the purposes of God in the earth. Amusing parlor tricks are not allowed. Just as Jesus did not turn stones into bread in Matthew 4, we should avoid the temptation to misuse spiritual authority or power. As we progress with God's master plan, we can act as spiritual traffic cops. We can blow a whistle, lift a white-gloved hand and make sure our team has the right-of-way.

The second principle is that of unity. In Matthew 18:19–20, Jesus says, "Again, I tell you that if two of you on earth agree about anything you ask for, it will be done for you by my Father in heaven. For where two or three come together in my name, there am I with them." If we're unified in God's assignment for our church, we are unstoppable. The Church's destiny will be lived out to the fullest in an atmosphere of unity with purpose.

Psalm 133 paints a powerful picture of authority and community in the Kingdom of God:

> How good and pleasant it is when brothers live together in unity! It is like precious oil poured on the head, running down on the beard, running down on Aaron's beard, down upon the collar of his robes. It is as if the dew of Hermon were falling on Mount Zion. For there the LORD bestows his blessing, even life forevermore.
>
> Psalm 133:1–3

God's empowerment always flows down from God's anointed senior leaders and not up from the people. We must align ourselves with the way He blesses versus building something we want Him to bless. God is no respecter of persons, as the Scripture says: "Then Peter began to speak: 'I now realize how true it is that God does not show favoritism but accepts men from every nation who fear him and do what is right'" (Acts 10:34–35). This means that there is no one in the world better or more important than you are. You are valued.

Despite our individual value, the Lord has created us to perform certain specific purposes. God has an agenda in the earth today and He is a respecter of function. That is to say that He wants to give us favor, opportunity and blessing to achieve His unique objectives. If we do not connect with His purpose, we block our own external blessing and internal peace.

When the Lord wants to have an impact on a region, He raises up leaders who will spearhead the movement. In the Old Testament, God used Deborah to lead the nation in a time of great uncertainty (see Judges 4–5). She and Barak worked in such close unity as leaders that it released a corporate anointing upon the entire team.

In the New Testament, the Day of Pentecost was marked by a unity that allowed a corporate anointing to manifest. When Peter stood up among the Twelve in Acts 2, he was the point man for a movement. He was not better than the other leaders, he was simply the man chosen to preach and lead the movement.

By the time the fledgling Church got to Acts 6, she realized that the apostles had to attend to their unique roles while releasing the work of serving tables to others. Thus deacons were created in the local church. As the Church organized itself in a way that permitted the corporate anointing to flow, exponential growth occurred. The senior leaders (apostles) had to connect with middle managers (deacons) while serving the needs of frontline managers (the Church at large). The corporate anointing comes from God alone. Our church visions must be seen as specific mandates from God. This mandate must be observed and then adhered to.

God's empowerment is neither derived from popular culture nor from a democratic process. Popular opinion alone is not the best barometer of God's will. If you look at places in the Bible where the people voted or decisions were made in deference to popular opinion, they often moved in error. The crowds, for example, wanted to crucify Jesus. Leadership teams, such as eldership groups, deacons and ministry heads should serve as safety nets if they are led by a man of God with a "consultative" leadership style.

My intention is not to get off into a discussion of church government. I simply want to assert that we must return to God's plan, despite numerous failures. There are indeed many places in the Bible where leadership moved in error. God's response, however, was to rebuke or remove the leader, not dismantle the divine chain of command.

David, the man described in the Bible as being "after God's own heart" (Acts 13:22), revealed the heart of God in his attitude toward Saul. He recognized the anointing from above even when the king was corrupt. David was determined to remain in right relationship with Saul regardless of Saul's offenses. If relationships are not right among people at all points in the chain of command, the anointing and enabling of God cannot flow in its fullness. If we as members of a church or ministry observe major character flaws, sin or doctrinal errors among the leadership team, we may consider finding a place where we can serve with confidence.

No earthly organization is perfect, yet God calls us to walk in harmony. Romans 14:19 says, "Let us therefore make every effort to do what leads to peace and to mutual edification." Paul says this to remind us of the big-picture issues of the Kingdom of God. When believers cannot serve together in peace, something is wrong. We need to resolve our tensions. Although I do not advocate church-hopping, sometimes the answer is simply to change churches. We should seek the Lord's guidance to join a church to which we can make a long-term commitment. We must avoid slipping into a consumer mindset, which simply views the church as a teaching center, organized for our personal preferences and convenience. Sometimes I have seen people overstay their welcome, in the name of being faithful. Typically they feel bonded to some of the members, but fail to understand the power of unity. These folks are often in danger of becoming bitter and disillusioned.

Most organizations cannot be reformed from the bottom up. Martin Luther is a classic example of this point. Luther originally intended to study law. After a harrowing near-death experience, he came to believe that God had a special purpose for his life and became an Augustinian monk in 1506. Ordained a priest just one year later, this zealous young theologian was shocked by the widespread corruption among the higher clergy. His early response to the problems in the Roman Catholic Church of the time was simply to preach and teach the truth as he saw it. His colleagues at Wittenberg supported his teachings and church life was very peaceful.

Things changed when a man named Tetzel "preached an indulgence in which crude theology was accompanied by the crassest materialism."[4] Luther could not take it any longer and he posted 95 theses for debate on the door of the local castle on October 31, 1517. Although Luther wanted to reform the Roman Catholic Church, which he loved, his vision ultimately led to the Protestant Reformation.

Luther's life shows us that reformers do best when they create new structures for ministry. Each generation has only a few genuine reformers, but God does call some people to this unique role. A pitfall for our generation is that we can mistake our preferences for God's priorities. If we slip into this trap, we could find ourselves inadvertently fighting God-ordained leadership.

Creating a Fresh Destiny in God

On a less serious note, I want to encourage you to find a church with a philosophy of ministry that you can connect with in a heartfelt manner. Having joy in the journey is necessary. It is actually a sign that we have fully connected with our destiny. Yes, we will have seasons of challenge, but we must continually return to our sense of purpose with passion.

The emphasis in America is always upon the independent individual. In some sense, we Americans are all cowboys out there riding the range all by ourselves. "The American Dream," as it is called, has always been about what the individual can become, and rarely is it related to a community or the nation and then only as it can provide a place for individual growth and success. American Christians bring that cultural perspective into the Church. Their major concern is often on what God can do for them—how they can be blessed. In contrast, the culture of the Kingdom is a place where authority flows down from above into a community characterized by unity, commonality and love. This powerful sense of community develops in a place where people adopt a vision, not just for themselves, but also for what they can be as a whole. On such a community, God commands a blessing and an authority that is richer and more powerful than we could have ever received as individuals.

Psalm 133:3 says, "For there the LORD bestows his blessing." So then, where is "there"? It is the place where the people of God embrace Kingdom concepts: (1) they see themselves as a community with a vision of who they are and what they can be together and (2) they submit to the authority of the King of kings and recognize it as flowing down from above through God's chain of command. God wants to pour out His blessing in our midst, but we have to deal with these two issues to prepare ourselves to receive it.

The problem with this discussion about mobilizing the Body of Christ at the local level is what some people might call the "super hero" leadership myth. Too many of us are waiting to follow a leader worthy of support instead of helping to create a fresh destiny in God.

Time and time again, I have seen people go from being actively engaged to mere passive bystanders because they saw themselves as being either a leader or a "dumb follower." We really do not want the Kingdom of God to be filled with people who cannot think for themselves. Even worse are those who feel as though the headaches of the ministry are for the paid professional. Too many people require an inordinate amount of direction and details. They are afraid to venture out or to take risks.

To move into your personal destiny, you must be totally involved in God's work. I am not talking about spending all your time at the church. I am talking about the spirit in which you approach your duties.

In *The Power of Followership,* Robert Kelley offers cogent thoughts on what it means to be a follower. The book, incidentally, has a very revealing subtitle, *How to Create Leaders People Want to Follow . . . And Followers Who Lead Themselves.* Kelley believes that:

> Exemplary followers balance . . . two seemingly mutually exclusive requirements. They have to. Independent thinking without active engagement can lead people with great ideas to fall short of implementing them or to become smart cynics who harass the leader. Active engagement without independent thinking can lead to yes-people who uncritically accept orders, whether good or bad. But exemplary followers who use both these skills become enormously valuable to leaders and their

organizations. Many leaders will go to great lengths to attract and accommodate exemplary followers because their contribution is both different and better.[5]

The principles we are describing can work outside of the doors of the church. In fact, the story of Ray Kroc, McDonald's famous CEO, is very inspiring. It shows that we can change at any age and become major contributors. Further, your contribution does not have to start from a position of high-level power or authority.

In 1955, Ray Kroc connected with the McDonald brothers as a franchising agent. Before this job, he had been a very average traveling salesman. At the time he joined McDonald's, he had just left a job selling milkshake machines. Kroc had moved from job to job, leaving no notable legacy until he turned 52 years old. Somehow, his imagination was captured by this new fast-food chain. Kroc moved from underachiever to the winner's circle. He expanded the number of stores from thirty to two hundred.

Although we remember him as CEO of McDonald's, in the early days he was content to make the McDonald brothers rich. No one would ever have envisioned his future role at McDonald's. When his peers began to reach retirement age, he was entering the most dynamic personal growth phase of his life.[6]

You and I must believe that we can have an impact for God in our generation, whether in the Church or in the marketplace. The only thing that can hold us back is a negative attitude. I am not talking just about an attitude that does not express faith in the Word. I am referring to a worldview that sees only pulpiteers as ministers. This philosophy dishonors the work of Calvary in the average Christian's life.

Conclusion

Every believer will have to make his peace with his "rank" or sphere of influence in the Kingdom of God. Our minds must be renewed to see things clearly. Some cultures can actually further obscure the biblical principles I have shared in this chapter. As an American, I have had to ask the Lord to remove some blinders from my eyes.

One of the redemptive gifts Americans have to offer the Body of Christ is their entrepreneurial initiative. But there are also elements of our common historical and cultural experience that are stumblingblocks. The United States of America is the "land of the free and the home of the brave." One of the early flags of the republic underscores our sense of independence. It shows a snake with these words written underneath: *Don't Tread on Me.* In summing up his feelings about the colonies' relationship with Great Britain, a member of the Virginia House of Burgesses, Patrick Henry, said, "Give me liberty or give me death!"

Our founding fathers discarded the concept of the divine right of kings and state control of the Church and, along with these, their traditional identity as Englishmen. They created an independent, constitutional republic in which freedom of speech was guaranteed and the establishment of a state Church was prohibited. This became the pattern and example for the rest of the world. What they did in the political realm was, to say the least, remarkable and revolutionary. They rejected the notion that civil authority comes down from above, but rather asserted that it is derived from the people. It is a political philosophy that is, as Lincoln put it, "government of the people, by the people and for the people." The character traits of self-reliance and independence are truly a part of the intrinsic makeup of our national consciousness.

The positive good that our independence has given to us is inspirational, but there is a problematic side as well. As Americans approach the idea of church leadership, they often bring beliefs loaded with baggage from the political realm. Yet there is a fundamental difference between American civil government and church government. The Kingdom of God is ruled by a King, Jesus, and authority flows down from above. Church leadership, therefore, is to take its cue from the Bible, not from prevailing political ideas of the day.

12

Maximum Impact

Happily Ever After

> If you know the enemy and know yourself, you need not fear the result of a hundred battles. If you know yourself but not the enemy, for every victory gained you will also suffer a defeat. If you know neither the enemy nor yourself, you will succumb in every battle.[1]
>
> Sun Tzu

Although spiritual hand-to-hand combat may be needed from time to time, the basic nature of our fight is more than simply casting out devils. My point in this book is that there is a larger battlefield. The writings of Neil Anderson and others have alerted us to the fact of invisible puppeteers (pulling equally invisible strings) creating very real problems in our lives.

As noted in the table of contents, waging spiritual warfare can be broken into three major divisions:

- The Warrior's Inner Life (chapters 1–4)
- The Warrior's Relationships (chapters 5–8)
- The Warrior's Corporate Connections (chapters 9–12)

First, we looked at the personal life of the warrior. We explored everything from "Love with an Attitude" to "The Character of a Christian Warrior." These four chapters have prepared you to have the peace and joy of God despite the opposition you may be currently facing.

Second, we discussed how to protect the significant relationships in your life. As you are being moved into a strategic position to serve the Lord's agenda, opportunities will typically open up for you through these important relationships. You multiply your personal impact through the pivotal relationships God gives you. Christian churches, businesses and families are typically only as strong as the relationships forged in each arena. As you learn how to truly walk in covenant with both God and your brothers and sisters in Christ, breakthroughs will be inevitable.

The third division of *The Warrior's Heart* laid out a way to think about corporate life. First of all, we studied the concept of discernment. Without battlefield "intelligence," the spiritual insight that God alone can give, you may connect with the wrong people. Some may take advantage of you. But with the right support systems you will be able to do the kind of tremendous exploits we touched on in chapters 10 and 11. It is clear that the Lord plants believers in specific churches because of the contribution that the church is supposed to make in that believer's life.

With these principles in mind, we can move safely from strengthening the personal life of the warrior to building lasting relationships and finally reaching maximum impact through corporate anointing.

The ancient Chinese military strategist Sun Tzu, quoted at the beginning of this chapter, offers ideas from the secular world that might be useful for Christian warriors as well. According to him, there are five essentials for victory:

- He will win who knows when to fight and when not to fight.
- He will win who knows how to handle both superior and inferior forces.
- He will win whose army is animated by the same spirit throughout all its ranks.
- He will win who prepared himself, waits to take the enemy unprepared.
- He will win who has military capacity and is not interfered with by the sovereign.[2]

He will win who knows when to fight and when not to fight. If you know yourself well, if you can truly address issues of your own character, you will know the right time to wage war. Peace and joy will be the hallmarks of how you operate.

He will win who knows how to handle both superior and inferior forces. As you gain perspective on relationships through trust, respect, understanding and expressed love, you will be able to flush out the true enemy. There will be no shadowboxing. More importantly, God can lead us by His divine strategies into lasting victories regardless of our resources.

He will win whose army is animated by the same spirit throughout all its ranks. Esprit de corps is a valuable asset in any battle. It is what keeps the military machine alive, racing toward its objective. We must recognize how the corporate Body of Christ connects to form an invincible army. This is a part of our birthright as Christians.

He will win who prepared himself, waits to take the enemy unprepared. Whenever we think of character-building, we think of hard work. Most people envision an experience like going to the dentist. It is a necessary but painful stop. But there is no quick path to victory. You must prepare your inner life while you wait for the big job to open up or the right mate to come along. Faithfulness is a virtue that is always high on God's agenda. Finally, after all this preparation, we must seize our moments. Take bold steps and move in faith.

He will win who has military capacity and is not interfered with by the sovereign. Every spiritual warrior is drafted into the King's army. If you are alive, you are assigned a rank and offered training. If you reject the war, it will still come and you will lose. This book has been written to develop your military capacity. God expects us to be good stewards of His grace. In addition, we must advance His cause in a way that does not grieve His heart. The Bible says clearly in Proverbs 6:16–19 that there are seven things God hates. We must avoid all of these. Yet there is one root attitude that seems to provoke Him the most—pride. "God opposes the proud but gives grace to the humble" (1 Peter 5:5). If you train and prepare with humility, the Lord will grace you with many victories.

Let me close with a story that illustrates our need to be vigilant, to recognize that we are at war.

It was during a time of civil war, fifty years before the birth of Christ. The soldiers of Julius Caesar were battling the forces of Pompey, a rival general, for control of the Roman republic. It was one of history's classic campaigns.

Caesar was the clear underdog. In fact, Pompey had more than twice as many troops and his cavalry outnumbered Caesar's by seven to one. During the long winter of 48 B.C., Caesar made a mad dash to the strategic port of Dyrrhachium, in modern day Albania, for supplies. But Pompey beat Caesar to the city. Blocked in his desperate bid for food, Caesar sought peace with his rival, an appeal Pompey rejected. "Dyrrhachium was one of the rare defeats in Caesar's career, which he readily admitted: 'Today my enemies would have finished the war if they had a commander who knew how to win a victory.'"[3]

Fortunately for Caesar, Pompey did not attack his exhausted and hungry army. He seemed instead to be in an analytic mode, puzzling on how to conduct what appeared to be a mopping-up operation. He did not decisively end the conflict, though he had the men, the food and the momentum on his side. What Pompey did not have was the burning desire to win—at all costs. For Caesar, though, time was running out.

The conflict was finally settled at a remote corner of Greece called Pharsalus. Caesar knew he had to create a strategy that would allow him to beat a superior force. Caesar also knew that, with the right plan, Pompey's prideful reliance on his cavalry could lead to his downfall.

Caesar lured Pompey's cavalry into a trap and created so much chaos that the cavalry could not use its superior numbers effectively. Then Caesar brought his own cavalry to bear against Pompey's unsuspecting footsoldiers. It was like releasing tanks on men armed only with handguns. Thousands of Pompey's men were killed or taken prisoner. The remainder of his once-massive force just fled. In the end, Caesar's troops actually captured more men than they had in their own army.

Pompey escaped on horseback in the aftermath and eventually reached Egypt, where he sought allies and fresh troops. But it was a doomed effort. A Roman renegade assassinated him there, and his head was later given to Caesar as a gift. There is a certain irony to Pompey's demise. Once the leader of thousands, he was killed by a solitary soldier. When we lose at the strategic level, any low-ranking soldier can kill a general.

In this piece of human history I see a parallel to the spiritual struggles of the Church. Like Pompey, we have already been given all the resources to win the battles before us. We must strive to use them more effectively. And we must never take our spiritual foe for granted, as he did. Like Caesar, we must press on even when times look dark. We may often feel outnumbered, yet we must persevere. Jesus did not say that we would be defeated. In fact, He prophesied boldly that the gates of hell would not prevail against the Church (see Matthew 16:18).

Although Satan's power was taken away at Calvary, he has not called it quits. He relies on the strategies of trickery and deception. They can be deadly; our enemy knows that we could win every skirmish if we knew better how to fight.

I believe that you and I are part of a generation of people who will answer the call to arms. As more and more Christians strengthen their inner lives, develop their relationships and understand the power of their corporate connections, we will see a mighty advancing of the Kingdom of God. Our fields of battle may be in offices or schools, in politics or the marketplace—wherever God assigns us. We will not stop until our world is transformed.

Be of good courage. You serve in God's army. You are a champion, part of an elite unit. You have a warrior's heart.

Notes

Chapter 1: The Warrior's Heart

1. Viktor Frankl, Nazi Death Camp Survivor, as quoted in Nelson's *Complete Book of Stories, Illustrations, and Quotes* (Nashville: Thomas Nelson, 2000), 36.

2. Major-General Carl von Clausewitz, *On War*, 1.1, 1832, tr. Michael Howard and Peter Paret, 1976, as quoted in Greenhill's *Military Quotations* (London: Peter G. Tsaouras, 2000), 515–516.

3. John Dawson, *Taking Our Cities for God* (Lake Mary, FL: Charisma House, 1989, 2001); *Healing America's Wounds* (Ventura, CA: Regal, 1991).

4. George S. Patton, rallying American troops in Britain, June 1944, as quoted in Torricelli's *Quotations for Public Speaker*, edited by U.S. Senator Robert G. Torricelli (New Brunswick, NJ: Rutgers University Press, 2001), 259.

Chapter 2: Honor Code and Conscience

1. J. Oswald Sanders, *A Spiritual Clinic* (Chicago: Moody, 1958), 60, as quoted in Nelson's *Complete Book of Stories, Illustrations, and Quotes* (Nashville: Thomas Nelson, 2000), 143.

2. Donald Grey Barnhouse, as quoted in *1001 Great Stories and "Quotes,"* compiled by R. Kent Hughes (Wheaton, IL: Tyndale, 1998), 74.

3. *Tristram Shandy* by Sterne as quoted by G. Campbell Morgan, *The Westminster Pulpit, Vol. X* (Grand Rapids: Baker, 1954–1955), 38.

4. James Madison, "Property," *National Gazette*, March 27, 1792.

5. Spiros Zodhiates, *The Complete Word Study Dictionary* (Chattanooga: AMG International, 1992), 1339.

6. Edmund Fuller, *Thesaurus of Anecdotes* (New York: Crown, 0–1942), 50–51.

7. Morgan, *Westminster Pulpit*, 41.

Chapter 3: The Warrior's Inner Strength

1. Anonymous, *He Paid a Debt*, © 1976 Soro Publishing. ARR.UBP.CCLI #130845.

2. Zodhiates, *Dictionary*, 737.

Chapter 4: The Character of a Christian Warrior

1. Patrick Henry (1736–1799) in his famous "The War Inevitable" speech, March 1775.

2. Gordon Dalby, *Healing the Masculine Soul* (Nashville: W Publishing Group, a division of Thomas Nelson, 1988), 122.

3. Winston Churchill, "We Shall Fight on the Beaches," speech to the House of Commons, June 4, 1940.

Chapter 5: Marching with Mutual Trust

1. SMA Glenn E. Morrell as quoted on http://medtrng.com/janldrshipquotes .htm (12 April 2003).

2. Stephen E. Ambrose, *The Victors, Eisenhower and His Boys: The Men of World War II* (New York: Ambrose-Tubbs, Touchstone by Simon and Schuster, 1998), 351.

3. Ibid, 354.

Chapter 6: The Inner War

1. Alphonse Karr, French author (1808–1890).

2. http://wesley.nnu.edu/John Wesley/methodist/ch7.htm; access 5/3/03.

3. Ibid.

Chapter 7: Friendly Fire

1. F. H. Bradley (1846–1924), British philosopher, *Aphorisms*, quoted in *The MacMillan Dictionary of Quotations* (Edison, NJ: Chartwell Books, 2000), 583.

2. Jed Diamond, *Male Menopause* (Naperville, IL: Sourcebooks, 1997).

3. Ed Wheat and Gaye Wheat, *Intended for Pleasure* (Grand Rapids, MI: Baker, 1997), 123–24.

4. Neil T. Anderson, *Victory over the Darkness* (Ventura, CA: Regal, 1990), 159–160.

5. Chuck Swindoll, *The Mystery of His Will* (Nashville: Word, 1999), 46.

Chapter 8: The Code of Confrontation

1. Father Nick Gosnell, chaplain to 16th Air Assault Brigade; March 16, 2003, www.military-quotes.com/Iraq.htm (12 April 2003).

2. Dr. Henry Cloud and Dr. John Townsend, *Boundaries* (Grand Rapids, MI: Zondervan, 1992).

Chapter 9: Intelligence and Infiltration

1. Lieutenant-Colonel Ralph Peters, *Army Times*, 24 August 1998, as quoted in *The Greenhill Dictionary of Military Quotes* (London: Peter G. Tsouras, 2000), 301.

2. Zodhiates, *Dictionary*, 1471.

Chapter 10: Corporate Destiny

1. Major-General John A. Lejeune, 1929, as quoted in *Greenhill Dictionary*, 447.

2. Robert S. McGee, *The Search for Significance* (Nashville: W Publishing Group, a division of Thomas Nelson, 1998), 11–12.

3. Adam Clarke, *Clarke's Commentary* (Nashville: Abingdon, 1824), 91.

4. Billy Graham, *The Holy Spirit: Activating God's Power in Your Life* (Minneapolis: Grayson, 1978), 213.

Chapter 11: Command and Commanders

1. Brigadier-General S. L. A. Marshall, *The Armed Forces Officer,* 1950, as quoted in *Greenhill Dictionary,* 326.

2. www.cbsnews.com/stories/2003/04/15earlyshow/main549420shtml.

3. Henry and Tom Blackaby, *The Man God Uses* (Nashville: Broadman and Holman, 1999), 104.

4. J. D. Douglas and Philip W. Comfort, editors; Donald Mitchell, associate editor; *Who's Who in Christian History* (Wheaton, IL: Tyndale, 1992).

5. Robert E. Kelley, *The Power of Followership* (New York: Doubleday, 1992), 126.

6. Ibid, 120.

Chapter 12: Maximum Impact

1. Sun Tzu, *The Art of War,* 3, c. 500 B.C., tr. Giles, 1910, as quoted in *Greenhill Dictionary,* 502.

2. Ibid.

3. Julius Caesar, *Appian, II,* 62, as quoted in *The Siege of Dyrrhachium, 48 B.C.,* http://heraklia.fws1.com/battles/Dyrrhachium/Index.html (2 June 2003).

Index

Harry R. Jackson Jr. is senior pastor of Hope Christian Church located near Washington, D.C. The ministries of this growing church, which consists of more than 22 nationalities and/or cultural groups, include a Bible college and an active missions program that sends worship and teaching teams to various nations.

Bishop Jackson's teaching ministry has taken him to Bible schools, leadership conferences and churches throughout the United States and abroad. His ministry revolves around two major focuses: personal communion with Christ and leadership development.

Bishop Jackson earned a B.A. in English from Williams College and an M.B.A. from Harvard Business School. For his work in Bible schools and churches domestically, he was awarded an honorary doctor of divinity by Christian Life School of Theology. He has been consecrated a bishop by the Fellowship of International Churches (FOIC). The FOIC vision, in part, is to promote the restoration of Kingdom reality in the marketplace and to prepare the Church for a revival of holiness. Part of its mission is to reconstruct society through church planting and making multicultural disciples from each generation.

Bishop Jackson, whose first book was *In-Laws, Outlaws and the Functional Family,* has been married to his childhood friend Michele for 25 years. They have two daughters, Joni Michele and Elizabeth.

THE HOPE CONNECTION

Harry and Michele Jackson are pastors of Hope Christian Church, a multi-racial, multi-cultural, local fellowship in the greater Washington, D.C., area. Their hearts' desire is to help others come into God's destiny through inspiration, instruction and impartation. The following is a sample of ministry they have conducted in the U.S. and other countries:

- The Warrior's Heart Workshops
- In-laws, Outlaws and the Functional Family Seminar
- Women or Men Retreats
- Leadership Training

For Further Reading: other books by Harry Jackson and V. Michele Jackson

- *In-laws, Outlaws and the Functional Family* (Regal Books)
- *High Impact Churches: Faith Lessons from the African-American Church* (TBR 7/2004)
- *How to Fireproof Your Job: Spiritual Help for the .Com Generation* (The Hope Connection)
- *Radical Praise: It's Not Just Business as Usual* (The Hope Connection)
- *Where the Rubber Meets the Road: Surviving and Thriving in the Midst of Chaos* (The Hope Connection)

For bookings, videos, audio tapes and CDs, contact The Hope Connection at:

Web site: www.thehopeconnection.org
E-mail: info@thehopeconnection.org
Phone: 240-206-0111
Address: The Hope Connection
Box 505
College Park, MD 20240
U.S.A.